MEMORIES...

OF A FAILED FOOTBALLER
AND A CRAP JOURNALIST

Hope you enjoy the book.

PAUL HINCE

Best Wishes

Paul Hince

EMPIRE
PUBLICATIONS

EMPIRE
PUBLICATIONS

GW00496709

First published in 2009

EMPIRE PUBLICATIONS
1 Newton Street, Manchester M1 1HW
© Paul Hince 2009

ISBN 1 901 746 54 2

Cover design and layout: Ashley Shaw

Printed in Great Britain by

D.B.P., Milton Keynes, Bucks.

To Anne and the Locusts,
Thanks for putting up with me

CONTENTS

FOREWORD

"**M**r Royle, you are the new manager of Oldham Athletic Football Club, on a one year contract and your first task as manager will be to meet the press upstairs."

Chairman Harry Wilde's first words to his new manager were followed with the warning, "and there is one of them who has got it in for this club in general and me in particular, so beware of Paul Hince".

I set off down the corridor to meet this journalistic ogre. Fortunately I was accompanied by the club's young company secretary, Tom Finn, who had a word in my ear en-route.

"Don't worry, Joe. Hincey's fine but he is a close pal of Jimmy Frizzell (the previous manager) and was very supportive of him".

On arrival in the press room I was met by Paul. "Hi Joe, welcome to Boundary Park. This is a smashing club, you'll love it here!". He was right and from day one Paul was equally supportive of me as he had been to my predecessor.

I had known of Paul as a player, even though he was from the football generation before me. I very quickly found out of his allegiance to his first club, Manchester City. Our daily contact to inform readers of the *Manchester Evening News* regularly ended with a brief discussion of the always entertaining goings on at Maine Road.

The press room at Boundary Park was an old store room that

had been converted to give 'Her Majesty's Press' some respite at half-time and full-time from the biting cold and inclement weather at Ice Station Zebra.

After every game Paul would greet me at the door of his 'press hut' and in his unofficial role as King of said hut, would ask the first question to the rookie manager to steer me in the right direction.

"Played well today!" or "Not the best today!" or "Lots of scouts here today, Joe!" All these pointers were eagerly grasped as I learned how to handle the post-match press conferences.

Thank you Paul for your support and friendship during our times together at Oldham. If I say that you are 'old school', it's meant as a compliment - meaning quite simply that you could be trusted.

Good luck with the book, weasel - I can't wait to read it!

Joe Royle,
February 2009.

INTRODUCTION

WHEN I ARRIVED in 1993 to take the reins at Manchester City, the national media had already begun to question the wisdom of my appointment. Although I had been in the game as a player and manager for many years and knew how the media worked, I was still a little taken aback by their vitriol and negativity.

Fortunately for me, however, there was one exceptional individual working at the *Manchester Evening News* at this time, who was not prepared to pre-judge and whose knowledge of the club and the game was clear to see. Over the coming months and during my tenure at the helm of Manchester City, Paul became a trusted and loyal friend.

As the first and only Chief Sportswriter for the *Manchester Evening News*, Paul carried out his work with utmost professionalism and integrity. Football managers are used to getting severe criticism and a battering from the media, especially during the tough times when results don't go your way. It often seems that few bother to get their facts right or take a balanced and constructive view.

Paul could never be accused of this. Maybe this has something to do with his deep understanding of Manchester City Football Club and what it means to support the team. It is surely also because Paul played the game before moving into the world of journalism.

A little known fact, but one he has reminded me of on many occasions, is that he played in every division in the football league during his career and scored in every debut he made! Someone whose career had taken him to Crewe, Bury, Charlton and his beloved City, clearly possessed something extra to most who make a living out of our great game.

At times, this meant that he would ask the question that others would be unable to see and be truly able to appreciate what actually happens behind the scenes, at the training ground or away from the glamour and excitement of the big match.

We have remained close friends and confidants over all of those years since my earliest days at City. I am delighted and honoured to have been asked to write a few words for Paul's book. I am sure that the stories and events recorded here will capture the imagination of all who follow Manchester City and of those who want to know more about the reality behind the headlines.

Brian Horton
February 2009.

PROLOGUE

I'VE NEVER WRITTEN a book before, even though I've been asked many times to do so. My excuse has always been that I'm too impatient to spend weeks and weeks writing an autobiography that may not even be published. The real reason is that, basically, I'm a lazy sod.

But after much badgering from family, former colleagues and Manchester City fans (and the odd United one) I've decided to give it a go.

I am writing these words by hand (having binned my laptop when I retired as the chief sportswriter at the *Manchester Evening News* four years ago) in the lounge of Hince Mansions, in the Garden Village of Hazel Grove, a leafy enclave about four miles outside Stockport.

At my feet sits my Stafford Terrier cross breed 'Scruff'. She is only three and looks mystified by what I'm doing. She has never seen me do a moment's work in her life. She has absolutely no idea what I'm doing, but there again neither do I.

So here we go, I'm going to sit here every day for God knows how long and put down everything that comes into my head. I've no idea what the finished product will read like but at least writing this book will keep me off the streets (and off the Murphy's) for a while.

IN THE BEGINNING...

PRETTY ORIGINAL way to start a book this, isn't it? But real writers start their books at the beginning so why shouldn't I? Crumpsall Hospital, Manchester, was where I came into the world on the 2nd March 1945 (nifty birthday eh? 2-3-45).

I was born into a large family (or so I thought) but more of that later. To all intents and purposes I had a father Tom, a mother Elizabeth, brothers Alfred, Thomas, Peter and Barry and sisters Joyce, Elizabeth, Margaret and Cecily. There were no tellies in those days which probably explains the number of kids. Somehow, before I arrived, they all managed to live together in a small terraced house in Ward Street, Openshaw - it must have been a case of first up, best dressed...

However before I was born one of the last bombs of the Second World War landed smack bang in the middle of Ward Street. No-one was injured but the houses suffered structural damage. The council's housing department relocated us to 1029 Hyde Road, Gorton - one of five huge, rambling properties with Far Lane opposite and Tan Yard Brow to the left. As I was growing up there was a working farm down Far Lane and a working tannery on Tan Yard Brow. How times have changed and not for the better in my book.

There is little in my early childhood which is likely to interest you, so I'll keep this part short (who's that who just said "Thank

God!"). My first school was Old Hall Drive Primary School. I wasn't the sharpest knife in the box, but somehow I passed my 11 plus exams which meant that the remainder of my education would be spent at a Grammar School. My mum chose Burnage Grammar which, in those days, was considered to be bettered only by Manchester Grammar in academic quality.

Burnage Grammar was a boys-only school and the discipline was strict. I remember being whacked across the head by a sadistic gym teacher named Mr Todd for being two minutes late. In fact, it was the bus from Gorton that was two minutes late!

'Sweeney' Todd had a large whistle attached to his hand; it was the whistle that made contact with my head. Within moments I had a huge lump on my temple. When I got home, Mam took one look at me and went ape-shit. It didn't do to make Mam annoyed; she would have given Frank Bruno a good fight. The next day she marched into school, sought out 'Sweeney' and, without a word, punched him in the eye. Oddly enough he never laid a finger on me from that day on.

In those days although I loved football, I adored cricket and still do to this day. I was a good little cricketer, even if I do say so myself - good enough to be made captain of the schools under-13 side. And it was in that role that I performed my greatest sporting achievement.

Manchester Grammar was - and still is - considered to be one England's greatest cricketing schools. They have produced a stream of England players and captains down the years - the last one being Michael Atherton. I led out my under-13 side onto the immaculate square at their ground and we slaughtered them. Batting at first wicket down I was given out on thirteen, to a delivery I didn't even offer a stroke to. It was two feet wide of off-stump. The umpire at the far end - a Manchester Grammar teacher - gave me out and I committed the unforgivable sin of refusing to walk.

In the end I had to go, of course, and waiting for me was our cricket coach, Mr Satherswaite. What a bollocking he gave me, my ears were ringing for hours. Many years later I wondered if "Satch" had also taught Sir Taggart - well he must have learned the hairdryer treatment from someone.

The next morning at assembly the Headmaster, Tom "the strap" Hughes, invited the team on to the stage. He praised and thanked us for bringing such honour to the school; he then told the entire school that they could go home and have the day off! Nothing I have achieved since has given me as much satisfaction, a four foot six inch schoolboy felt six feet tall that day.

That wouldn't be the last time I was paraded before a full assembly at Burnage - but the other occasion was far less auspicious. Right from day one I had been a cheeky little beggar, and that hadn't changed when I entered my final year. Along came the important GCE exams and there was one exam I was dreading above all the others - algebra. I had just not been able to grasp the subject.

When I opened my exam paper, all my worst fears were confirmed, I couldn't even understand the questions, never mind come up with the answers. So I sat there for an hour or so with a blank paper staring back at me. The teacher in charge of the exam did his rounds, to make sure no-one was cheating, and stopped when he got to my desk.

"Hince," he said sternly. "Why have you answered none of the questions?"

"Because I don't know any of the answers," I replied.

In a whisper he then said, "At least put your name at the top of the paper, you will get a two percent mark for that."

"What if I put my name on the paper fifty times," I replied, "will I get one hundred percent for that?"

You won't be surprised to hear that I was ordered out of the exam room and told to report immediately to the Headmaster to tell him what I'd said. I knew what was coming when I revealed my cheekiness to "Strap-em-all" Hughes. Out came the dreaded implement of torture, six lashes to one hand, and six to the other. It was a school record up to that point and I felt quite proud of myself. But there was more to come.

At the following morning's assembly, I was ordered onto the stage where Headmaster Hughes pointed an accusing finger at me and informed the whole school that P Hince, Form 5 Alpha, had become the first scholar in the school's history to achieve nil percent in a GCE examination. Well at least I'd found my way into Burnage Grammar School's history book - not a lot of pupils do that!

*

OUR NEXT-DOOR NEIGHBOURS in Gorton were Mr and Mrs Wilson who had two children - Maureen and David. Maureen was in her twenties but Dave was the same age as myself and we became firm friends. He was certainly peculiar looking - as tall and thin as a latt. If he turned sideways you'd mark him absent.

As I've already mentioned there was a working tannery on Tan Yard Brow and one evening Dave and I decided to raid it. In the tannery's grounds was a small forest and bonfire night was approaching so we decided to relieve them of a few trees. Of course it was private property surrounded by a huge fence and we knew that if we were caught we would be charged with trespass and theft - but we didn't give a toss.

We waited until the tannery works shut for the day and began our raid. Armed with axes we crept down Tan Yard Brow and scaled the fences. For the next hour of so we chopped away to our heart's content - it was pitch black when we headed home with our booty. I was first to scale the fence as we made good our escape. Unfortunately I fell straight into the burly arms of a waiting copper wearing a face like a bag of spanners. The next thing to come over the fence were the two axes thrown by Dave - the first axe chopped off the bobby's toe cap - the second took a huge chunk out of his policeman's helmet.

We were in the shit now! Trespass, theft and assaulting a police officer - the slammer was beckoning, it never dawned on me that 11 year-olds didn't get banged up. The copper caught Dave as he fell off the fence and then he wrote our names in his little black book. We were absolutely terrified. What would mam and the rest of the family say when they realised they'd been harbouring an 11 year-old master criminal all this time?

Worse was to follow: the bobby frog-marched us home and told our respective parents what we'd been up to. I don't know what Dave's punishment was but I was placed under house arrest for seven days. No radio (TV hadn't arrived in our house as yet) no comics and only bread and water to eat. Take my word for it - being a master criminal was not all it was cracked up to be.

Nutty Dave next door was mad about chemistry. The original nutty professor if you like. He ended up as one of the leading scientists at ICI so he obviously knew his onions. One day he called for me and told me that he was going to show me something horrific. He took me upstairs to his bedroom where his two white mice, Alice and Bob, shared the accommodation.

There, lying dead at the bottom of the cage in a pool of blood, was Bob. During the night Alice had gnawed off Bob's feet. I blamed Dave for not feeding them. Anyway Dave decided that Alice had to stand trial for murder in the first degree. I was to be the judge and Dave the Prosecutor - for such an open and shut case we decided that Alice didn't deserve a defence.

In the absence of any mitigating evidence I had no option but to judge Alice guilty as charged. I put a piece of black paper on my head and sentenced her to death. The only problem I had was how to despatch Alice to the Big Cage in the Sky. Dave got me out of difficulties by offering me his chemistry genius. We decided that Alice was going to be exterminated by gas chamber.

Dave's sister Maureen had bought him a chemistry set for his birthday so he went to work mixing all sorts of mysterious potions. He warmed them over his mini bunsen burner until a toxic green cloud began to drift up. Then he poured the concoction into Alice's cage.

The devious little madam refused to die. She kept coughing out clouds of green gas but she stubbornly refused to peg out. I changed my verdict rapidly . "Death by hanging" I ruled. Dave brought out this ball of string and we slipped a noose around Alice's neck. Holding onto the string we threw her out of the bedroom window - the houses were four storeys high, if the hanging didn't kill her the fall surely would.

Dave's sister Maureen ran a one-woman hairdressers on the ground floor of 1027. We were three stories above her but still heard the screams as a white mouse attached to a piece of string dangled outside her window. We saw one of her clients bolt down the road with her curlers still on shrieking blue murder.

We had obviously ruined Maureen's business but to make matters worse, Alice still wouldn't do as she was told and die. We decided against throwing her on the fire - we thought that was a touch cruel. We tried to drown her and discovered she could swim. We buried her alive and she dug herself out. So we gave up and took Alice back to the pet shop - that was fifty years ago! It wouldn't surprise me if she was still alive today!

TWO MOTHERS

YOU MAY RECALL that I mentioned before that I had been born into a large family - or so I thought. I'd better explain that confusing statement so I can get on with the book.

When I was very young - probably four - my 'sister' Margaret took me to one side and told me that she was my real mother. A four year-old can't comprehend that sort of situation, so I merely shrugged my shoulders and got on with life - this time with two mothers. Not long after Margaret and her husband Arthur left 1029 Hyde Road and moved into a bungalow in Abbey Hey.

I continued to believe that I had two mothers for the best part of fifteen years (I told you I wasn't the sharpest knife in the box). When I told my best mate Jimmy Grindey that I had two mothers, he looked at me as though I was stupid.

As time passed, and after the penny had dropped, the resentment for my natural mother grew. Whatever the circumstances, how can a mother abandon her baby? I asked 'brother' Peter why every member of the family had gone along with the deception for all these years. He told me that 'Mam' had sworn them all to secrecy - and you let 'Mam' down at your peril.

For many years after that, I never spoke to my natural mother or even saw her. That suited me fine. At the age of nineteen, I married my childhood sweetheart Susan at St Chad's Church in Ladybarn. Out of courtesy I invited my mother to the wedding. She attended but I never said a word to her either before the service or at the reception afterwards.

Much later, when Susan and I were living in Hazel Grove, I would visit 'Mam' often. My mother used to pop in often as well. When she walked into a room, I walked out. I wanted nothing to do with her.

That deep-rooted resentment lasted for over fifty years. Then it began to dawn on me that her husband Arthur was dead by now, and she was living in a council flat in Burnage - ironically only a throw-in away from Burnage Grammar. It struck me that you only had one mother and bearing a grudge was pointless.

On impulse, on the way home from work one afternoon, I knocked on her door. She nearly dropped cork-legged when she saw me. She was now in her seventies, but she was still a handsome woman. That first meeting was what the acting profession call "the theatre of embarrassment". It was excruciating. I didn't know what to say to her and she didn't know what to say to me but at least the ice had been broken. With each visit after that she told me a little bit more about how I had come into this world.

According to her the war was on and Manchester was swarming with American troops. There was an American camp on the outskirts of Manchester, which housed thousands of soldiers. You know the old war time saying about the yanks being "over-paid, over-sexed and over here," well the second part of that saying definitely applied to my mother.

She was a WREN in the army, God knows what WREN stood for (woman's royal something or other). Anyway one night, she went to a dance at the American base, and fell in love (at first sight) with an American named Frank. The obvious happened.

I never knew that people used to have sex outside of marriage (this was 1944 remember) but apparently the art of horizontal jogging with the first person you met was as prevalent in 1944 as it is in 2009.

The rest I don't need to tell you. Mother told me that she conceived at the first attempt. If you believe that, I'm Alex Ferguson's long lost son. So then I knew. I was half-American. If I had my choice I'd rather be poked in the eye with a rusty nail than be half-American. I have never tried to make contact with my father. All I know about him is that he came from a wealthy family in Utah (must have been a Mormon) and that when he knocked up my mother he was a married man with children.

When my mother went to the base to pass on the happy news to my "adoring" daddy, he didn't want to know. The American authorities sent him home, back to his wife and kids in Utah, and awarded my mother a pram. Thanks very much America! If I ever see an American flag I'll spit on it.

Of course by now I understood my mother's reasons for giving me away. These days, young girls get pregnant just so they qualify for a council flat, which they don't have to pay for. In 1945 it was the opposite, becoming pregnant made you a social pariah. An unmarried, pregnant girl was shunned by the neighbours. She brought shame on the family. The entire family would have been spurned by their friends. So shortly after my birth, my mother handed me over to her mother. I was officially adopted by Elizabeth and Thomas Hince.

Do I understand why my mother let me be adopted? Yes. Do I really forgive her for giving away her baby boy? No. Social stigma? Ignored by the neighbours? Who cares. The greatest sin in the world is to abandon your child. When my mother told me that I was conceived after only one night of passion with Yankee Frank, I didn't believe her. What are the odds on that?

Some years later my brother/uncle Peter, told me that my true mother had given birth to a second child, by the same shag happy American soldier. Peter told me that the new born was a girl. Not bad going that is it? Two romps under the blanket and two children. Just as well mother and "daddy" Frank didn't stay together, they would have ended up with 38 kids.

So there I was in my late fifties, and I'm suddenly told that I have a sister. Peter told me that he saw "Mam" leaving 1029 Hyde Road with the baby in her arms. Where she went, I have no idea. I suspect the baby - my sister - was smothered at birth. In those days that was the tragic fate for babies born out of wedlock but there's a chance she was adopted.

Many times over the last few years I've thought of trying to trace my sister. But where do you start? All I can say is that my mother's married name was Bristow and my sister would be in her early sixties - there is a million to one chance, but if she falls on this book by mistake, I would love her to make contact.

Right, I've got that off my chest so I'll return to the main story, which I know you're dying to read! (As if).

JOURNALISM AND CITY BECKON

A FTER LEAVING Burnage Grammar School at sixteen, I had a job to find. Deep down I wanted to be a doctor - and eventually a heart surgeon, I could have stayed at school and taken my 'A' levels but that would've led to two more years at school followed by another six at university and medical college.

I couldn't do that to Mam. By that time the only breadwinner in the house was my brother Jim. The family needed another wage earner. But Mam told me to go for it and study to become a doctor. For the one and only time I disobeyed her - my second occupational choice was to become a journalist and that's what I set out to do.

I walked to every local newspaper in the Manchester area - no point in approaching any of the daily "fish-n-chips" rags because they would never employ a sixteen-year old straight out of school with no journalistic experience and, to their credit, they all gave me an interview.

The *Ashton Reporter, Sale Guardian, Stockport Times,* they all interviewed me but the answer was always the same -we have no vacancies but we will keep your name on file. I didn't believe a word of that so I answered an advert from a local textile company named A.G. Leventis based on Oxford Road in Manchester. Naturally I passed the interview this time! I was going to be trained (for five years) as a textile buyer. The company's market was in Africa, the plan was that when I learned the business I would be posted to either the Nigerian capital (Lagos) or the Ghanaian capital (Accra).

I couldn't wait to reach twenty one to qualify for my African adventure! As it turned out I remained in the textile industry - working towards completing my training - for an impressive four days. A career in journalism soon called, one of those local papers had kept my name on file.

On the Thursday of that week there was a knock on the door of 26 Lindleywood Road in Fallowfield (our new address) and on the doorstep stood a man called Dennis Middlehurst. He was the editor of the *Gorton Reporter* which was part of the Ashton Reporter Group where I had gone for an interview. Mam invited him in.

I had never seen her so courteous and hospitable. She ushered Dennis into the "best" room and brought in tea and biscuits - Dennis would've preferred a large scotch, but I didn't know that at the time. He seemed impressed that I had visited every paper in Manchester and he offered me a job on the local *Gorton Reporter* with a princely salary of £2 7s 6d, new technology has passed me by so you'll have to work out what that would be in today's money yourself but it's probably about 30p.

Needless to say, I accepted the offer without a second thought, the next day I told my gaffer at A.G. Leventis that I was going to leave. He didn't even give me a week's notice. He looked up to the heavens - tutted loudly - and told me to go home. So at the age of sixteen I became a journalist - of sorts.

I reported for duty the next day and immediately discovered that the staff at the *Gorton Reporter* consisted of editor Dennis, and two other "cub" reporters called Graham Tait and Colin Bell (honest!) and a black cat called Lucky. Whoever named that cat was having a laugh. He had one ear, a leg missing and he couldn't open his right eye properly, he ponged to high heaven and couldn't control his bowels. God knows what it would be like to be trapped in a lift with that 'lucky' cat!

The three cub reporters were given an area to cover, my patch was to be Gorton, West Gorton, and Openshaw. And I had no idea that the world's gaze would soon be focussed on this area within weeks of my arrival at *The Reporter*.

My first major assignment came less than a week after I joined the newspaper. All of the big Sunday papers had reported the disappearance of a young lad named John. He and a friend called Tommy had gone climbing in the Lake District. The weather was atrocious. Tommy had found his way back down from the mountains, but of John there was no sign.

A major rescue operation had been launched – the Mountain Rescue had been called and three RAF helicopters were scanning the area. What interested my editor was that John lived on my patch in Gorton. Dennis already had John's address – near Mellands Playing Fields – and asked me to visit the family.

"Be very tactful," he cautioned, "just explain that you are from their local paper and politely ask for a photo of John – just remember their son is almost certainly dead."

I walked to the address Dennis had given me and knocked on the door – there was no answer. I knocked again and I could hear footsteps as the person on the other side of this huge thick piece of timber approached. A boy of around twelve or thirteen answered.

"Can I speak to your parents?" I asked.

"Sorry," he replied "they're both at work."

"What's your name?" I asked.

"John," he replied.

I stood there bewildered "But you're supposed to be missing somewhere in the Lake District!".

"No," he replied, "I got split up from my mate in the fog so I walked down the mountain and got the train home."

I walked back to the office. "Hmm," I thought, "what a waste of time."

Dennis the editor met me at the door. "Did you get a picture of the lad?" he asked.

"No point - there's no story there."

"Why not?" asked Dennis.

"Well, there is no story there because the lad is at home," I replied.

Dennis's face turned pale "No story?" he spluttered "No story! Half the country is scouring The Lakes and he's sat at home in Gorton and you say there's no story- I have a good mind to hand you your P45!"

Okay you may think that story is funny, but that dressing down taught me a lesson. Sometimes in journalism you have to see the story behind the story, you have to think on your feet - and at sixteen, me and the art of thinking were distant strangers. Clearly I still had a lot to learn before I could call myself a journalist.

★

MY OTHER MEMORY of working for the *Gorton Reporter* is a dreadful one. What an awful introduction into journalism I had as a sixteen year-old rookie as I tried to cope with a story which was front page news all around the world.

I refer of course to the days when this great city was smothered by evil. Like my colleagues from other newspapers I spent an entire year trying to find evidence that might help to convict the inhumane Moors Murderers Myra Hindley and Ian Brady. Remember (if you are old enough) that most of the children abducted and eventually sadistically killed were from Gorton, West Gorton, and Openshaw - my patch.

I think I equipped myself fairly well. The police eventually arrested Hindley and Brady and revealed their names and addresses. It turned out that Brady was Scottish but Hindley was born and bred in West Gorton.

I worked out (from where Hindley lived) that she probably went to the local secondary school opposite Mellands Playing Fields, so I paid the school a visit.

I sweet-talked one of the teachers and she allowed me to look at the school register. There was the name I was looking for - Hindley. I wrote down the name of every one of her ex-classmates and their addresses. For weeks after I tramped around the streets of Gorton to build up a picture of Hindley as a young teenager by knocking on the doors of all her former classmates.

All the boys and girls of her year said the same thing: she was such a nice, normal girl. She would walk to a herbalist shop on Cross Street in Gorton to spend her pocket-money on diabetic chocolate for the kiddie next door. I even spoke to the boy who fondled her breasts down an alley alongside Gorton Monastery, "Sweet, kind and gentle", he told me.

Whether you are of a certain age or not, whether you were around at the time or not, you will all have an opinion of Myra Hindley. No doubt you will believe her to be a heartless, evil devil - which may be what she became - but in that year I got close to her without ever meeting her or speaking to her and, after talking to her former classmates, I still firmly believe that she was (and emphasize the word was) a normal considerate young woman who was corrupted by the devil's spawn, Brady.

*

MY CAREER WITH the *Gorton and Openshaw Reporter* (or the Backward Gazette as we called it) was still its infancy when I interviewed 'Bouncing' Billy Barker. Billy was a well-known local celebrity who never walked anywhere. Instead he jumped down the road in his wooden clogs, hence the nickname.

Bouncing Billy was incredibly old when I met him, he said he was born in the early 19th century which would have made him well over 150 when we spoke! So, mad as a hatter and a lying old git as well! Bill brought out his photo album and I glanced through the sepia images. On one photo I could just about make out a figure on a roof.

He told me that he used to entertain fans at City's Hyde Road Stadium by doing a clog dance on the roof of the main stand before the players took the field. One day he lost his balance and fell off the stand. From that height it seemed inevitable that Billy was on his way to meet his maker but a miracle occurred that Saturday. Instead of plummeting to his demise, Billy landed on an extremely fat woman who unwittingly broke his fall.

Billy was understandably delighted but not for long. Mrs Fatso may have broken his fall but that wasn't the only thing broken. Billy's portly saviour was rushed from the ground to the nearest hospital with a broken collarbone, a fractured arm and a bruised big toe! Clearly she would not be able to work for some considerable time and sued City for compensation. The Blues coughed up and told Billy to piss off - his clog dancing on rooftops came to an abrupt end.

Fortunately Billy had other claims to fame. He insisted that he could jump on an egg without cracking it and that he could leap in the Gorton canal and bounce off the surface to reach the other side. Rather foolishly we decided to put Billy's claims to the test.

Billy gave me an egg and an eggcup and told me to put the two together and set them down on the cobbles outside his house. This achieved Billy came bouncing down the road and launched himself feet first onto the egg. Splat! The egg burst and the contents splattered me from head to foot. A brand new shirt ruined. Jesus, I was going to catch it from Mam when I got home... and I was going to have to wash my hair - it was June and I wasn't scheduled for another bath until October...

The next day I accompanied brainless Bill to the banks of Gorton Canal. I took a photographer with me to capture the moment Billy performed his miraculous trick of jumping off the surface of the water. Billy counted out his run-up, turned and came bouncing in - he could certainly jump! He took off as if he had a rocket up his arse and reached the middle of the canal in one leap - put his foot on the water's surface and sploosh! He disappeared from view.

I just stood there watching. I thought it was part of Billy's act. Time passed and it dawned on me that Billy was probably one of those people who can hold their breath under water for an eternity. My photographer, meanwhile, was beginning to panic and soon so was I, so I ordered him to jump into the canal and pull Billy out. He told me to fuck off.

So it was left to me to save the old sod. I waded in and wobbled my way toward where Billy had landed. The canal stunk to high heaven and the water was up to my chin. I took a deep breath and ducked under the water - I couldn't see a thing, it was pitch black down there but I could hear something, it was a faint gurgling down to my right. I fumbled around and caught something, it was Billy's false teeth... at least I was getting close.

More fumbling followed and my hand found someone else's hand - fortunately attached to an arm. I took hold tightly and inched my way backwards. I scrambled out taking the hand with me and there attached to it was the spluttering Bouncing Billy! He was still alive, I think, although it was difficult to tell with Billy at the best of times. When he had finally stopped spewing out gallons of Devil's Piss do you know how grateful he was? He only asked me to go back into the canal to collect his false teeth, the cheeky twat.

So there we had it, two interviews with Billy and two sets of clothes ruined and a second bath in as many days! I never interviewed Bonkers Billy after that as I now realised that getting within 100 yards of that goofy geriatric was seriously harmful to my health.

*

IF YOU KNOW a journalist who claims he doesn't fiddle his expenses then you're keeping company with a liar. Every hack uses journalistic licence when filling out his expenses sheet. It's one of those little perks that everyone knows about including the editor (who is no doubt fiddling his own!) who turns a blind eye.

My expenses during those early months in the *Gorton Reporter* were typical. I would spend five shillings doing my round and claim £5. Okay. By today's standards that's peanuts but we are talking 1960 now £5 was a lot of dosh - remember I was only being paid £2 7s 6d for a full working week so it was twice my normal wage.

Then the accountants started running the business, as they do to this day. You think editors run our national newspapers? Think again. Every paper is controlled by the faceless number crunchers up in the dungeons who, when they are not robbing the poor hacks, have an enjoyable time pulling the legs off Daddy Longlegs.

One week my expense sheet was returned with a note from the accountant which said I had to itemise the expenses and produce receipts for every penny I claimed. All of a sudden I was £5 out of pocket! What to do?

Within hours I dreamt up a cunning plan. Every time I made a bus journey I would empty the ticket box by the door and by the end of the week I would have accumulated thousands of spent tickets. Next time I sent in my usual claim for £5 and with it I sent a huge envelope full of tickets. I knew the accountant wouldn't sit there for hours counting them and I was right. I duly received my fiver plus a note from the accountant to the effect that my expenses no longer required receipts!

Up at the *Reporter's* head office in Ashton there was an old journalist called Bill Johnson who in his prime had been quite a celebrity as Chief War Reporter in Europe for *The Times* between

1942 and 1945. I was having a natter about expenses with him when he told me a story which put my bus ticket scam in perspective. On arriving back at *The Times* offices in Fleet Street in 1945 Bill wasted no time in handing in his expenses claim. He simply wrote: "Coverage of World War Two = £30,000".

A few minutes later Bill was summoned back by his editor who told him that the accounts department would not sanction his claim. "Times have changed while you've been away, Bill," explained his editor, "you will have to account for every penny you spent over the past three years if you want your expenses."

Bill snatched the sheet out of the editor's hand and marched off. A minute later he was back with a new expense claim on which was written:

Taxi fare to and from Victoria Station = £20.

Coverage of the war £29,980.

And he got every penny.

"LAUGHING ALL THE WAY TO THE TITLE"

WHILST AT the *Reporter*, I played outside right for local teams such as RESEDA or Ladybarn Youth Club as a fully paid up member of the wingers union (one of the principal conditions being that you avoid any form of physical contact). I may not have been a big lad but at least I had pace. In those days I could give a greyhound a ten-yard head start and still beat it around the track.

By this time the scouts from the local professional clubs began to turn up to watch me play. I went for a trial at Bury. I played in their "A" team against Everton. The ground at Lower Gigg Lane was worse than those I had been playing on for RESEDA - it was a mud-bath. It was an effort to lift my feet out of the mud it was that deep. What a nightmare. Needless to say Bury lost their interest in me because I might as well have not been playing in that match. Little did I know that I would be playing as a professional with Bury many years later – unfortunately with about the same level of input!

In the weeks prior to my trial with Bury, I had noticed one man at all our games. Via our manager I found out that his name was Harry Godwin and that he was Manchester City's chief scout. I never thought he would recommend me to the Blues believing that he wouldn't be impressed by the fact that I smoked while I played (the honest truth) but he must have found out where I lived because postcards started to arrive signed by Harry asking me to come and play for City at junior level.

At the time I refused because I had no wish to become a professional footballer - I was a junior hack remember, with no desire to leave journalism - but crafty Harry bagged me in the end. He sent me one of his little cards imploring me to play for the "A" team on Saturday because City only had seven players available. If you think about it that's ridiculous but I believed him. I was accustomed to turning up for Ladybarn Youth Club or RESEDA matches to discover that only six or seven of my team mates could be bothered to play that day so I thought a professional club might occasionally run into the same problems!

Eventually I phoned Harry and told him that I would play on Saturday. The "A" team pitch in those days was in Urmston (enemy territory) and my eyes popped out of my head when I walked into the home team dressing room. There must have been thirty young players in there, so much for not being able to field a team!

Anyway, Harry had conned me into playing for the "A" team and had also arranged for first team coach Malcolm Allison to come down and watch me in person. To be honest I don't think I played that well that day. I managed to score a goal and we trounced the Rags four-nil, which is always a good thing.

Malcolm must have seen something in me because a couple of days later my phone at *The Gorton Reporter* jangled and a voice at the other end said "Hello Paul. This is Joe Mercer." For any reader under sixty I should explain that Joe Mercer was the Blues greatest ever team boss. My response to that phone call from Joe was to tell him to "piss off". I thought it was one of the lads in the office having a laugh. It was only when he gave me his private number at Maine Road that I took him seriously.

Joe's offer was that I should train with the other players at Maine Road on my day off and play six games for the reserves so that he could assess my potential. I agreed but my knees were knocking when I said "yes" to Joe. Playing in the Central League might sound like nothing these days but in those days the standard was awesome. Seventeen-year-old kids never played in the Central League. If I tell you that Manchester United, in the early sixties, fielded a reserve team for a Central League match that contained eleven current international players, you can see now why my knees were knocking. I just knew that I would be out of my depth.

My first game for City's reserves was ironically enough against United at Old Trafford. In those days the two clubs held mini-Derbies the evening before the main derby. Funnily enough I wasn't in any way nervous as I got changed in the away dressing room,. But I was terrified a few minutes later when I came out of the tunnel at Old Trafford. . . just a week earlier I was being watched by two dogs and a lost cat playing for RESEDA or Ladybarn.

All I saw as I walked onto the Old Trafford pitch was a sea of faces. I found out later that the official attendance that night was just over twenty thousand - who says pro soccer hasn't changed? An attendance like that these days for a reserve team fixture is unthinkable. Was I scared as I lined up for kick-off? Is the Pope Catholic? Put it this way, I was the only player on the pitch at that moment with dirty shorts on. And yes, the dirt was at the back and yes it was brown.

I remember little of the match itself. I vaguely recall that Stanley Bowles was making his reserve team debut that evening. He was the only City player I knew. He had played in the same team as me in his amateur days when we were both selected for the Manchester U21 Representative side. Oddly enough Stan played at outside right in that team and I played outside left. Odd because Stanley couldn't kick with his right foot and I only used my left foot to stand on.

Stan and I became firm friends during our time at Maine Road, and we remain so to this day. He even travelled up from London to be a guest at my second wedding to the beautiful Anne (well I had to say that, didn't I).

Back to that debut game at the ashtray with lights. I remember that we won 2-1 and that Stanley and I scored the goals. His goal was a screamer. Mine was a mis-hit shot - as usual - which just about crept over the line.

My only other recollection is of taking a corner at the Stretford End. As I was lining up to take the kick I was hit behind the ear by a small glass bottle of lemonade. Those Rags fans always have liked me. Did it hurt? You bet your bloody life it did. The blood was pouring down my back and it took a dozen stitches after the match to sew the gaping hole. But no way was I going to show those charming Stretford Enders that I was hurt, so I turned to face them and took a swig of the lemonade. "Thanks very much", I mouthed. I was feeling a bit thirsty, just as well it was real lemonade. I've peed into a lemonade bottle while at a football match! Well when you've got to go, you've got to go!

To be honest, I didn't think that I'd played very well in my first three trial matches, so to save embarrassing the Blues any further I wrote a note to Joe Mercer. I explained that I didn't want to play for City anymore. I must have been crazy. There I was, a fanatical City supporter, being given the chance to play for the Blues. A bit like a starving man refusing a plate of fish and chips. Joe's response was to ring me again and ask me to meet him at Maine Road immediately.

When I arrived he took me onto the pitch. He put his arm around my shoulder and walked me around the perimeter. I was soon to learn that whenever he had made a decision about a player - to drop him or play him - that is what he did, a slow amble around the pitch with an arm around that player's shoulder. What he said to me that day changed my life. As I was to find out Joe was a very wise counsellor, whose advice was always first class.

In a nutshell Joe said that he didn't know if I would make a good professional footballer but he said that if I turned down the offer he was about to make, I would regret it for the rest of my life. I would age into a bitter old man grumbling to his grandkids that "I could have been a contender". I knew instinctively that Joe was right. What convinced me even more was his offer. A two-year contract at £25 per week plus bonuses. That will sound like peanuts today but remember, I was earning £2 7s 6d at *The Reporter*.

Of course I snatched his hand off; I mean I'd never seen £25 in my life. I might be daft but I'm not stupid. So that afternoon I became Paul Hince the professional footballer, rather than Paul Hince the budding reporter.

Many times over the next few years I left Maine Road with tears streaming down my face because I had never laughed so much. Francis Lee later said that the team laughed its way to the Championship title - and he was dead right, as you will discover...

★

So LIFE BEGAN at Maine Road. By a country mile it was the best and friendliest of all the clubs that I graced with my presence. Friendships were quickly formed. I've already mentioned that I knew Stanley Bowles and within days of arriving I was a good pal of goalkeeper Alan Ogley, John Clay - a brilliant half-back who we nicknamed Cassius (Cassius Clay - get it!) and David Connor who was one of the finest defenders in the country.

Another good mate, scouser Tony Coleman, gave keeper Ogley the nickname 'Mr. Magoo' because he was almost blind and he had to wear thick bi-focal glasses like the cartoon character. Alan couldn't keep goal in his specs, so the club bought some special contact lenses which were as big as his eyes. Before training and matches he would pull out his eye lids with a little rubber sucker and ram in the contacts. Once in place the eye lids kept the contacts in place when he dived. Watching him perform this procedure always made me feel queasy.

Come a reserve team game at Wolves. What a dank horrible

night it was - drizzling, cold and misty, with an attendance like the ones from my amateur days - one man and his dog. The little box containing Alan's contacts were supposed to be in the team's skip, only they weren't. They had been left behind at Maine Road. Our coach, Dave Ewing, was beside himself. We had no substitute goalkeeper, in fact subs hadn't been invented in those days. What was he going to do? Mr. Magoo offered to play in his glasses. I told him that the ref would never allow that. So he just shrugged his shoulders and said, "Bollocks to it. I'll play without my contacts and without my glasses".

Typical of the Blues that isn't it! Playing a match with a blind goalkeeper! I offered to go and ask the ref to put a pea in the ball, and for some reason Alan was grossly offended.

"Are you trying to make out that I'm fucking blind?" he snarled.

"I'm not trying to make out anything," I replied. "You *are* fucking blind."

At one point during the match, Dave Connor spotted Alan talking to the goal post, thinking it was a team mate. On another occasion centre-half Mike Batty had to turn Magoo round because he was staring at the net instead of the pitch. We lost the game 2-0 and Magoo never realised that Wolves had scored.

As we sat in the communal bath afterwards, I looked around between puffs (yes I was still smoking, even though I was a pro footballer) and I couldn't spot Alan.

"Where's Magoo?" I asked of big Dave. "No idea," he replied.

"I suggest you go and look for him," I said. "With his eye-sight he might be asking the nearest chippie where the bath was."

Dave went onto the pitch and there was Magoo - still crouching and squinting into the fog, fifteen minutes after the game had ended. I was laughing all the way home. I've told that story a thousand times down the years and nobody has ever believed me. I told it at a City supporters meeting about a dozen years ago. Magoo had driven from his home in Barnsley, all the way to Stockport, to hear my over long and terminally boring speech. When we had a gargle afterwards (or two, fifteen and twenty-four). He agreed that everything that I had said about him was true. The only thing he denied was talking to the goal post.

"I thought it was Ian Mellor," he said. Good point. Ian in those days was as tall and as thin as a goal post. But as far as I know, he didn't go around attached to a goal net.

GENIAL JOE

THE LEGENDARY Joe Mercer should never have accepted the offer to manage Manchester City. He had suffered a stroke during his time as manager at Aston Villa and clearly hadn't recovered when he took over at Maine Road. Great that, wasn't it? A blind goalkeeper and a manager who, due to his condition, had the memory span of a goldfish.

From the day I arrived to the day I left, he called me Stan and Stan Bowles, Paul. But he was a wonderful character, nonetheless. Gentle, kind, and endlessly patient. A bit like Sir Taggart at the theatre of nightmares (as if!).

I'll give you an example of his management skills. My good friend David Connor had been at Maine Road for around four years when I signed for the club. By then he must have rattled up around sixty first team appearances. When I told him that my basic salary was £25 he was miffed and I didn't blame him - Taj was only getting £20, five pounds less than me, a raw recruit.

Taj was shy and didn't want to cause trouble but I urged him to go and see Joe for a pay rise. In the end I had to virtually frog march him to his office. Half an hour later he emerged with a huge grin on his face and I knew he had negotiated a good pay increase.

"How much more has he given you?" I asked.

"He gave me nothing," said the beaming Taj. So I asked what had gone on.

"I told the boss I had come to see him for a rise and he said that he had a big bag of money available but the big players (Lee, Summerbee, Bell etc) had come in before me - had taken a dip out of the bag - and there was none left for me."

"Well what the fuck are you grinning for?" I asked.

"Because he said his door would always be open to me," replied Dave. Open door, closed wallet. I know which I would have preferred.

I've already mentioned John "Cassius" Clay, a top class right half (midfielder) until he suffered two broken legs in training. Cas came back after a long time out with injury but he was never the same again. The two breaks had changed his running style. He was virtually running up and down on the spot. His legs were hitting his chin when he ran but he seemed to stay in the same place. So I made a pact with John. When he got tired in the "engine room", I would swap places with him. Like most wingers, I would be fresh as a daisy after 30 minutes because I ignored the ball at all costs. As a midfielder, Cas would be gasping for breath. The switch worked like a dream until one day Joe (the manager, if you've lost the plot) came to watch the reserves.

John and I had deployed the switch-of-position system for months and no one had said a dickie bird. But on that day we walked into the dressing room at half time to meet a manager with a face like a robber's dog. He ordered Cas and me into the treatment room and we both knew what that meant - the mother and father of a bollocking. I had never seen Joe like that. He was foaming at the mouth, he gave us the rollicking of a lifetime.

"When I pick you to play at outside right, you fucking well play at outside right," he spat at me.

"When I pick you to play at inside right," he yelled at John, "you fucking well play at inside right." I was chastened, but Cas burst into laughter.

"For Christ sake John," I said to him, "stop laughing while the gaffer is giving us a bollocking. What are you laughing at anyway?"

Behind his hand Cas whispered, "Look for yourself; he's got two ties on."

I didn't want to but I had to look. Joe was, indeed, wearing two ties. I laughed that much that I literally fell off the treatment table.

Joe halted his tirade.

"Here I am trying to bollock two of my youngest players and all they do is take the piss out of me," he said.

The door slammed and Joe was gone. I don't remember him ever watching a reserve team game from that point on.

Older readers may remember City's crown of jewels at that time included Francis Lee, Mike Summerbee, Colin Bell and, to a lesser extent, the vastly underrated Neil Young. Monday mornings for us was torture: running at Wythenshawe Park under the gaze of England's international long distance runner Derek Ibbotson.

Joe never watched us in training but one week he made an exception. The week before, we had noticed that the wind had blown over a tree on the road leading up to the park. Francis had a chat and, as we reported for training one morning, with Joe's other jewels Summerbee, Young and Bell he had hatched a plot knowing that Joe was coming.

Colin, Mike and Neil were loaded into Francis's new white Jaguar (FHL was the number plate if I remember. Francis' middle name being Henry) and drove towards the park, parking in front of the fallen tree. Then he drove up the leaning trunk, before yanking on the handbrake. The four stars then threw open the doors and lay outside with just their feet inside the car, as though they had had a serious accident.

A few miles behind, Joe was plodding along at ten miles an hour. He saw the stricken vehicle and the dead bodies hanging outside the car. As he drew nearer he recognised the car and realised his four 'crown jewels' were probably dead. In his state of health that was the last thing he needed. Whether Joe had another stroke, I have no idea. What I do know is that his old Morris Minor careered across the road, hit a paving stone, demolished someone's hedge, and ended up in someone's front garden!

The next story is about Malcolm Allison who, in my book, was the greatest coach this country has ever seen. One season in the FA Cup we were drawn against Blackpool in the third round.

In the first match at home, we paralysed them. We hit the woodwork nine times but ended up drawing 1-1. Goalkeeper Joe Corrigan was making his debut that day. Mike Summerbee finally broke the deadlock but a Blackpool midfielder, whose name I can't recall, equalised in the second half. His shot went through Joe's legs and didn't have the pace to reach the back of the net. It crawled over the goal line and stayed there. I could have kept it out with my willy but I wasn't going to say that to big Joe - he was about 8ft 10.

For the replay at Bloomfield Road, the following Wednesday, the club pushed the boat out and booked us into the magnificent Norbrek Castle Hotel. Coach Malcolm gave specific instructions. We could go out on the town on Saturday night, Sunday night and Monday night. On Tuesday we would go to one of the shows in the seaside resort and on Wednesday we would get ready for the match with a training session (drat!).

On Sunday we all went to a night club above a bowling alley. My last recollection of the night was seeing TC (Tony Coleman) flat out under a table being fed neat vodka by a fat slapper.

The following morning we staggered downstairs to see that the Norbrek was staging a furniture exhibition in the main reception area. All the sofas and chairs were under sheets and the exhibition was due to be opened by the Lady Mayoress of Blackpool. She whipped the sheet off a five seater sofa and underneath lay TC -

totally naked and with his false teeth slumbering on his chest. Lady Mayoress shrieked - us City players applauded.

After the match (which we won, of course) we celebrated in every pub in town then returned to our hotel as pissed as newts. At about three in the morning big Malcolm Allison shouts "who wants a drink?" A pretty stupid question if you ask me.

Malcolm rang the bell and a waiter appeared. He looked like something out of Dickens' Christmas Carol complete with long nightgown and a candle in his hand. Malcolm told him that he wanted the bar opened. The waiter refused. He said it was something to do with the licensing laws. Mal wouldn't accept that for an answer. He jumped behind the bar and ripped off the grill in front of the players. What he also did in the process was pull down all the light fittings attached to the grill. The damage must have run into thousands and for the next three hours we drank ourselves sober ten times – and it was all free.

Needless to say right up to this very day the Blues have never been invited to stay at the Norbreck Hotel.

*

DEREK JEFFRIES WAS a local boy from Longsight when he signed for City. He was as thick as a gypsy's tit but he was some player. He had ice instead of blood in his veins and was absolutely unflappable in any situation. I once told him that he had permission to panic but the words fell on deaf ears.

Even as a kid he was International Class. That was until coach Malcolm Allison publicly declared that the club had unearthed the 'new Bobby Moore' from which point Derek's career deteriorated.

For some reason Daft Derek always referred to me as 'Mister Hince' even though I was just 12 months older than he was. One day he plonked himself next to me in the dressing room and said "'ere Mister Hince, have you got a dog?"

I told him that I had a dog called 'Pippin' who I had bought from one of the pet shops on Tib Street for the princely sum of ten bob – the equivalent of 50p today.

A few days later Derek came running up and announced that he too had purchased a puppy from Tib Street. I asked how much he'd paid for it and he said twenty pounds. My jaw dropped open – no dog costs that much on Tib Street, they're all mongrels.

"Oh, it's the right price" added Derek, "the petshop owner told me it was a pedigree... 'A Tripehound'".

You may find that hard to swallow but I swear that it's true.

It might help you to understand how bonkers Derek was if I told you that his ambition after he ended his playing career was to buy a bank. When I questioned him about this his answer was blindingly obvious: "banks always seem to be busy".

The late, great chief scout Harry Godwin told me once what happened when he went to sign my mate Stanley Bowles who lived with his mum, dad and younger brother Keith in a pre-fab in Moston.

Harry and Stan sat down at the table. In a rocking chair near the fire sat Stan's mum drinking neat gin out of the bottle. Stan's younger brother had nothing but a vest on and was underneath the table removing the contents of Harry's pockets.

A standard form had to be filled in and the player's age, address, weight and so on were logged. Finally Harry came to the question of Stan's denomination. Stan, of course, had no idea what that meant. Harry told him the question was asking which religion he was. Stan scratched his head and shouted to his mum, "Ma", he said "Am I Kafolic or one of them there Prodistants?"

His mother put down her gin and replied "I don't know Stanley. You'll have to ask yer dad when he gets home from work".

Stan was only fifteen at the time but back in the sixties you could leave school at that age if you had a job to go to and the school agreed. Harry told me that after Stan had signed, he got a letter from Stan's headmaster thanking him for taking Stan out of school a year early!

In the reserve team at Maine Road we had a giant of a centre-half named Mike Batty - in truth he was a gentle giant who you couldn't offend... no matter how hard we tried! Stanley Bowles and I teased him constantly.

Our favourite trick was to have a quick shower after training and then, while Mike was soaking in the bath, we would put his clothes on before putting our own clothes over his. We would be peeping from behind a corner as he left Maine Road wearing his football boots because we had nicked his shoes and a borrowed Mac under which he was stark bollock naked. What the other passengers made of him when he caught the bus home I can only imagine.

At that time in the sixties, City's greatest enemy wasn't United but Leeds. And they hated us right back! It made no difference what level the matches were - first team, reserves, youth team - every match against The Tykes was a bloodbath.

One Saturday afternoon I played in a reserve team fixture against them at Maine Road. I knew it was going to be a typical Leeds performance when their full-back volleyed me into the Kippax - and that was before the match had kicked-off. Ten minutes or so into the second half I was about to take a corner when the referee beckoned me over.

"Count your team-mates" he ordered.

"Why, can't you count to eleven?" I replied.

"Just do as you're told and do a head-count" said the officious official.

So I did... "one, two, three, four, six, seven, eight, nine, ten... No that must be wrong." But I wasn't wrong, we only had ten men on the pitch!

"Have you sent someone off without us noticing?" I enquired, "because we appear to be a player down."

As the ref and I stood there trying to unravel the mystery we heard the sound of studs coming down the tunnel and Mike Batty trotted out. The ref beckoned him over and asked him where he'd been.

"For a shit," replied Batty.

"Well go and have a longer shit," said the ref, "because I'm sending you off for leaving the field of play without permission."

The first team centre-back at the time was George Heslop, a burly, amiable Geordie who had a handsome head of golden hair that he was forever admiring in the mirror. But his barnet was beginning to thin and by the time I left Maine Road for Charlton Athletic he was as bald as a coot.

I didn't last long at Charlton and was back in Manchester within two years when one day I bumped into George in St Ann's Square. Strangely all his hair seemed to have returned. I thought no more of it and didn't hear from George for a further two years until the phone rang one Monday morning and he was on the other end.

George was finishing off his career at Northwich Vics and wanted to know if the *MEN* were carrying a match report on their last match against Boston United. I told him that we were because I had just read the report. George's next question was a mysterious one. "What does the report say about me?" he asked. I told him, truthfully, that the match report merely said that he'd had an excellent game. George thanked me, said his goodbyes and that seemed to be that.

Unfortunately that wasn't that! Not when I saw our first edition which explained why George had phoned me and solved the mystery of his re-appearing hair. Nobody's hair grows back when you go bald (unless you're Stephen Ireland!) I was just too stupid to recognise that fact when I'd bumped into George, he was wearing a syrup.

What had happened during that match against Boston was that

George had gone up for a header and his wig had flown off. To make matters worse the Boston striker caught the syrup with a beautiful volley and rocketed it into the back of the net. Worse still the wig lay there in the netting fluttering like a dead pigeon in the breeze. To compound matters, a photographer had taken a picture of George's disembodied hairpiece hanging in the net, worse still that picture was on the front page of the *Evening News* that night.

When I got home from work the missus told me that George had phoned a dozen times. I wasn't surprised, I knew what was coming. I had no idea that we were carrying the wig picture that evening.

George did phone back and gave me the mother and father of all bollockings. He simply didn't believe that I had no hand in the syrup exclusive. He said his kids were ashamed to go to school.

I tried to cheer him up. I told him he would go down in history as the only man to score an own goal with his wig - George was not amused.

DEBUT DAY

As I SETTLED down in the reserve team, I started to play really well (if I say so myself). The only blemish was taking a penalty against Newcastle, at Maine Road, and putting the ball onto the roof of the Platt Lane stand - from 12 yards out that took some doing!

As that season progressed the full time training began to kick in. Although I had always been quick, I was now much stronger. I even chanced making the odd tackle. When Easter arrived and City faced three matches in as many days, there were a couple of paragraphs in the morning papers suggesting I could make my senior debut against West Brom at Maine Road on Easter Sunday. I didn't believe it, especially when I played in the reserve match at Bolton on Good Friday. But the following morning, Malcolm Allison rang to tell me to report to Maine Road at 2 pm.

"Don't worry," said big Mal, "you're not going to play, Taj has got a slight strain and I just want you there as a precaution." I should have known it was a ruse to stop me from getting worked up before the match. If I'd have a brain I would have sussed it out, Taj was a right back I was a right winger. No way in the world would Malcolm have played me at right back if Taj was declared unfit. I couldn't tackle my way out of a paper bag.

Yet I fell for Mal's line and was nerveless when I reported in at Maine Road. Like the other players I just passed away the time by glancing at the programme, taking a stroll around and working my way through a packet of cigs. Then at quarter to three, Malcolm came into the dressing room and said to me, "Scoop get changed because you're making your debut today."

I had what might be described as a better than average debut. I was marked by West Brom skipper Gareth Williams, who was also captain of Wales. Oddly enough he marked George Best when he made his debut for the Rags. I scored twice in the space of sixty seconds - they were both sitters. The West Brom keeper, John Osborne, palmed out two shots from Neil Young straight into my path. I couldn't miss.

Between those two goals I missed another absolute sitter. I don't know where Osborne had got to when our Scottish striker, Ralph Brand, picked me out with a perfect cross. I could have brought it down and tapped into the empty net. I could have chested the ball in, but no, I had to showboat with a spectacular header and missed the ball completely.

We still had a two goal advantage at half time but, typical of the times, we let them back into the game, which ended in a 2-2 draw.

My esteem for West Brom skipper Williams, soared that day. He was hard but fair. He was built like a brick shit-house and could have booted me into the main stand if he wanted to. But in the entire 90 minutes he never fouled me once. He was the first to congratulate me on my goals at the end of the match. He said I had played fantastically well on my debut and wished me many more games like that. Our own manager, genial Joe, didn't share Gareth's sentiments - he dropped me for the Easter Monday game at Leicester!

On Easter Monday I reported to Maine Road and noticed two young girls standing on the steps that led up to the main entrance. When I got out of my car they came running over.

"Excuse me," said one of the girls. "Can I have your autograph please?" Oh, oh. I thought. This is the start of the Paul Hince fan club.

"Certainly, my dear," I replied. "What's your name?" To which she replied, "Deidrie".

So with a theatrical flourish I wrote "To Deidrie. Love and kisses from Paul Hince." As I gave her back her autograph book and walked away, I heard Deidrie's pal say, "See, I told you that wasn't Colin Bell." And in response, Deidrie tore the page from her book, ripped it into little pieces, and threw them into the gutter. Doesn't half bring you back to earth, something like that!

I didn't play another first team match that season although I was often picked for the first team squad. Just being in the squad qualified you for first team bonuses, based on home attendances. I was in the squad when that season's derby took place at Maine Road. The crowd bonus alone was £150 - an absolute fortune to a player with a basic wage of £25. Plus your pay automatically rose to £50 when on first team duty. So there I was at nineteen, suddenly earning £200 a week. If I tell you that a measured mohair suit cost about £5 in those days, then you can work out what a huge sum £200 was. It would probably be the equivalent of £7-8000 today.

Even better, the crowd bonus carried over to away matches. We faced four successive away games after the derby. And Joe told me that I would be in the senior squad for all four. That would have meant £800 for me to add to the £200 from the derby. A thousand pounds! You could buy a house for that much in those days. And do you know what I did? I begged Joe to let me return to the reserve team and he agreed. I must have had a slate loose even then.

I wasn't selected for the first team squad for the rest of the season, but scored goals galore for the reserves. I knew that I would get another chance sooner or later. But what I didn't know was that my City career was drawing to a close before it had really started.

★

A FAVOURITE DRINKING spot for the City players in the sixties was the Piccadilly Club not far from the Gardens in the city centre. Wednesday night was boy's night out and Stanley Bowles and I were picked up by Tony Coleman for our night out on the town. Being a regular in the first team 'TC' was considerably richer than Stan and I and drove around in a flashy American car.

That night in the Piccadilly Club the three of us got as pissed as the proverbials. Me and Stan knew that when we'd had enough – we'd fall over. But 'TC' had no 'stop valve' when it came to drinking – he boozed until he was in a coma. By three in the morning Tony could barely stand up but he insisted on driving us home. That might sound crazy now but remember there were no breathalysers in those days. So we fell into 'TC's' car. What a fanny magnet! Long bench seats ideal for shagging and the back seat looked almost threadbare – Tony had obviously done some horizontal jogging on that!

So off we went in the general direction of Moston – me next to Tony with Stan fast asleep on the shagging bench behind. Five minutes into the drive I was sober enough to realise that 'TC' was driving the wrong way up a one-way street. Before I had chance to warn him we were side-swiped by a double-decker bus heading for Wythenshawe. No one was injured but Tony's car lost one of its back doors. Stan was snoring and seemed blissfully unaware as Tony sped away from the scene.

He was cornering like Stirling Moss – at one stage Stan shot out of the car like a rocket but fortunately he landed on grass! 'TC' and I had to manhandle him back into the car. Stan was still asleep or maybe dead! We were about half-a-mile from Stan's pre-fab when Tony spotted a croft. We abandoned the car and legged it leaving sleeping Stan to face the music.

Two odd events occurred after that crash. Firstly, Stan never mentioned it the next day at Maine Road, presumably he woke up every morning in a car with its back doors hanging off. And secondly, 'TC' never heard from the police. Obviously in Moston a flashy American car abandoned on a croft with no back doors and a professional footballer asleep inside must be a common sight!

★

THE SEASON AFTER I made my debut started badly for the first team at Maine Road. After four games we had accumulated just one point and were propping up the First Division. I had taken up where I left off the previous season. After the second team's fourth match we were top of the central league, and I was averaging a goal a game. Not bad for a chicken-hearted winger.

I didn't go banging on Joe's door demanding a place in the first team. One, I've never had a forceful nature – if I was any more laid back, I'd be horizontal. And two, Joe was as honest as the day is long. He didn't have favourites and I knew my chance would come again. I was picked for the next match at Coventry and I scored again. I also laid on goals for Nijinski Bell and Nellie Young. I was reasonably satisfied with my performance, but the Sunday morning papers went completely over the top.

One paper declared that in me, City had unearthed the new Jimmy Greaves. Ridiculous! Jim was a legend in those days for Spurs and England, I wasn't even a household name in my own house.

The papers had just started marking the players' performance. Two of the Sunday papers awarded me ten out of ten. Two more gave me a nine, and every paper had named me man of the match against Coventry. Bollocks! I played okay but there were better City players on the pitch against Coventry. I wasn't flattered by those marks or the man of the match ratings. I was downright embarrassed. I knew I would be in for some ribbing when I went to work the following day.

Many of the players must have decided to arrive early at Maine Road. They formed a Guard of Honour outside the main entrance, and applauded me all the way to the dressing room. My face was bright red for the rest of the day. Many years later when I was the *Evening News* City reporter, the paper introduced the player marking system. I hated them as a player and I hated them as a journalist. Before they were introduced I simply didn't mention in my match report anything about a player who'd had a stinker - now there was no hiding place. Each player had to be given a mark. The lowest was four and the maximum was ten. I knew the marking system was going to cause trouble between me and the City players - and it did.

I travelled with the team to Ayresome Park for a night game against Middlesbrough. Fans of a certain age will remember that this turned out to be the wonderful Paul Lake's last appearance. After only five or six minutes he was taken off after a recurrence of a cruciate ligament injury. Tragically he never recovered - a tragedy for him and a tragedy for England because prior to the initial injury he was set to be the England captain for many years to come.

Anyway, back to the marks. City were abysmal that night. They wouldn't have beaten the blind school. I had no choice but to set the marks low. A couple of days later I drove to City's old Platt Lane training complex to interview Tony Coton. The moment I parked up I was confronted by City's scouse midfield enforcer

Steve McMahon.

"You fucking twat," he growled, "I've a good mind to stick one on your massive hooter."

"What's the matter with you today?" I asked, "has the missus refused you a leg over again?"

"I'll tell you what's up with me," he spluttered. "It's those fucking marks. You gave Lakey six points and I only got four and he was only on the pitch for a couple of minutes. How do you explain that you slimey little rat?"

"That's easy Macca," I replied. "I gave you four, because I'm not allowed to give anything lower."

Macca was happy with that.

"Oh, that's alright then," he said, "come upstairs and I'll make you a cup of tea."

I wasn't going to risk any more opportunities for a City player to break my nose, so I hatched a masterplan. From then on in I allowed the players to award their own mark. After every match the players were brutally honest - sometimes too cruel on themselves. A player would often give himself a four when I would have awarded a six. The only one who didn't co-operate with the marking system was clown-prince keeper Coton. Well he did co-operate in a way. After each match he would award himself a mark of eleven! Anyway back to my playing days...

After making ten consecutive appearances for the first team, the run ended with a 1-0 defeat against Arsenal at Highbury. I knew the axe was coming. Malcolm had asked me to mark the Gunner's winger Geordie Armstrong that day. What I didn't know was that Geordie had a rocket up his arse. He ran the legs off me. If I touched the ball once, I can't remember it. Still I hadn't done badly for a kid. When I played my first game at Coventry, we were bottom of the league. When my run of appearances ended, they were top of the old first division. I scored five goals over those ten games, and scored another three in two FA Cup matches. If I had been playing today that would have been recognised as a fantastic goalscoring ratio.

That was the season, of course, when the mighty Blues won the English championship. You would have thought I qualified for a championship medal, wouldn't you? But I never got one. When I hung up my boots years later, I had only one medal - that was for being runner-up for Charlton in a London reserve league which contained four teams. I threw it away the day after I received it.

Life carried on merrily in the reserves at Maine Road but approaching Christmas I was hit by a bombshell when the Blues signed Francis Lee from Bolton Wanderers. As I said before, I'm daft but I'm not stupid. I knew that my City career was as good as over. Francis had been signed for £60,000 (a colossal figure in those days). He was also a right winger. I was just a local kid. I was never going to oust Francis from the first team - unless I pulled the pin and dropped a hand grenade into his pocket. I knew I had to leave.

I asked Joe for a transfer. He refused point blank. He even offered me a huge pay rise to stay. Then I explained my reasons for wanting a transfer. I told him I wasn't interested in money (liar) but simply wanted to have regular first team football. He relented and told me I could leave.

So I was placed on the transfer list which is sent to every club. I must have had some admirers because the chief scouts of a host of clubs flocked to watch me play. Three clubs made me an offer - Aston Villa in the First Division and Second Division clubs Bristol City and Charlton Athletic. Of the three, only one made an acceptable bid - Charlton. What they offered was the princely sum of £37,500. Peanuts by today' standards, but a large amount in 1967.

Once again genial Joe offered me more money to stay, once again I refused. So a couple of days later I was told that the Charlton manager, Eddie Firmani, was waiting to meet me in the Midland

Hotel in Manchester's city centre.

That evening I went to meet Eddie. He asked what I wanted to drink and I said a pint of bitter. I should've known he wasn't a full shilling when he got himself a glass of water. How can anyone drink something that you wash in? The meal in the Midland was excellent but Eddie raised an eyebrow when I lit a Rothman's. I suspected then that trouble was around the corner.

Eddie asked me how much I wanted to join Charlton. I told him £45 a week basic and he nearly had a heart attack. For the next few hours he was on the phone to his chairman Michael Glickstein (giving me the chance to get tanked up at his expense). Finally he came back and said that his chairman had agreed to my demands.

So aged twenty I became a Charlton player. Malcolm and I took the train to London and waiting for me outside the main entrance in his blue Mercedes was Eddie.

He dropped me at the Westcombe Park Hotel and he hadn't said a word to me on the 15-mile journey. I had the nagging feeling that I had made a grave mistake in joining the Addicks.

In hindsight, leaving City when I did was just that. They say you don't know what you've got til it's gone and that was certainly true in my case. I may not have been made for Manchester City but Manchester City was made for me.

I had been a supporter of the Blues all my life and the years at Maine Road were far and away the happiest of my playing career. As mistakes go, leaving City at such a young age is the equivalent of the blunder made by the Decca record producer who refused to sign The Beatles because he believed that guitar bands had had their day.

The question is – how might my career have developed if I had remained at the club? The facts are that Francis Lee didn't play in every match in the second half of that championship season, so there would certainly have been a chance to play in the extra three or four games which would have earned me a championship medal, I certainly wouldn't have thrown that away. What a wonderful leagacy that would have been to hand down to your kids and their kids.

One thing is certain, from being a park footballer, Joe Mercer and Malcolm Allison had moulded a player good enough to play in the top flight of English football. I know I would have improved still further if I had my put my trust in Genial Joe and Big Mal.

Who knows, perhaps I really could have been 'a contender' but I was too stupid to take the chance and it's a mistake I regret to this day.

I look back now and realise what a wonderful management team we had at Maine Road in Mercer and Allison. When they first teamed up in 1965 - Genial Joe, the wise owl and Malcolm, the young tearaway whose exploits off the pitch were already legendary, it had the potential to be a nightmare when in truth it was a union blessed by God. I left Maine Road a better person just by getting to know those two wonderful men.

The strange thing was that when Allison succeeded Mercer as manager in 1972 everything went tits up for him. Malcolm only managed The Blues for 43 matches of which just 14 were won before he walked out to return to his native London to take charge of Crystal Palace.

He was never as successful at the many clubs he managed after leaving City as he had been alongside Mercer at Maine Road. Perhaps he needed a wise counsellor at his side to curb his excesses all along.

As I'm writing these words, Malcolm's life is ebbing away, by the time you read them he may well have passed away, but I will remember him until my dying day for what he really was - one of the greatest coaches in the history of English football.

MY LONDON NIGHTMARE

THE MARRIAGE BETWEEN Firmani and me was damned from the start. He was a South African and a God-fearing Christian who hated smokers and drinkers. I was a heathen from Gorton, who smoked for Great Britain and drank enough to sink the Titanic. It was a disaster waiting to happen.

It got that bad that at one stage he would frisk me for fags before I climbed onto the team bus. It was like Miami Vice. He would spreadeagle my legs and order me to turn around and put my hands on the coach. I quite enjoyed it actually, particularly when his hands felt my erogenous zones. I always got on the coach with a lob-on.

What Eddie didn't know, of course, was that I'd given team mate Graham Moore my cigs to stash away. Graham and I always sat at the back of the coach and Eddie always sat at the front. So I could smoke like a trooper on those trips, and, with the window open, Eddie was none the wiser.

My debut for Charlton was against Plymouth Argyle at Home Park. During the previous evening at our hotel I had been taken ill. My throat was so sore that I couldn't swallow and I was so hot you could have fried an egg on my chest. I was petrified. I thought it was something terminal because of an incident which had happened when I was due to sign for Charlton.

After I had agreed terms with The Addicks, I was told to go for a medical at Lewisham General Hospital where a consultant named Dr Buck was waiting for me. As far as I was concerned everything went well during the medical. Dr Buck seemed happy with the results and said he just needed a blood test before going back to The Valley. I gave blood then drove to The Valley to put pen to paper. Believe it or not, my arrival had caused quite a stir. When I went into Eddie's office it was packed out with journalists and photographers.

The idea was that I would be photographed signing my contract. Suddenly the phone rang, Eddie listened for a few moments, and then snatched the pen from my hand. Then he told the reporters and cameramen to piss off. I asked him what was wrong, and he mumbled something about not being able to sign me. I wasn't going to let him get away with that and insisted that he told me the truth. Eddie explained that the phone call had been from Dr Buck and that I had failed my medical. It was the blood test which I had failed. Apparently there were more 'ureas' in my blood than in a dead man. Eddie told me I had no choice but to return to Maine Road.

The trip back from Euston to Piccadilly station was the longest and loneliest of my life. What was wrong with me? I wondered. And then it dawned on me. Leukaemia - a death sentence in those days.

City's chief scout, Harry Godwin, was waiting for me at Piccadilly station. He told me that an appointment had already been made with a blood specialist. His surgery was in Didsbury, close to the Christie Hospital. Then I knew - I had blood cancer!

The appointment was two days away and I couldn't wait that long. As soon as I got home I went to see my G.P., Eric Godfrey, who was an avid United fan but I didn't hold that against him. Because of my involvement with City, Eric and I had become firm friends and remain so to this day, although he must be about 225 by now. But I trusted Eric implicitly and knew that he wouldn't lie to me.

Even though it was late in the evening, Eric drove from Didsbury to Fallowfield and opened up his surgery (never happen today, would it?) and gave me a thorough examination. He drove me to the Jewish Hospital in Manchester where my blood was taken. He asked me what I had done before my blood test at Lewisham General. I told him I hadn't done anything. I had woken up with a thumping headache because the room was boiling. I was going to be late for training, so all I had for breakfast was four aspirin swallowed down with a cup of tea.

In a flash Eric knew what was wrong with me. I didn't have blood cancer at all. With no solids in my stomach after taking those aspirins, the pills had caused a false blood test. No, he assured me, I didn't have blood cancer - my blood was as pure as a newborn baby's. And I was free to join Charlton.

Early in my career at the Valley I still trained at Maine Road and travelled down to London by train every Thursday. I stayed at The Westcombe Park Hotel in Charlton and came back to Manchester on Saturday night. One Thursday morning I was sitting on the London train at Piccadilly Station with a handful of other passengers when, looking out of the window, I spotted a stunning blonde walking along the platform - she had tits like melons and her arse looked like it was chewing caramel when she walked.

A few minutes later this vision appeared right in front of me and plonked herself down. I thought that this was a bit odd seeing that the train was half-empty but hell, who cared, I would be ogling those knockers for the next three hours - what a way travel.

Her name was Janine, she was 32 and recently divorced. She lived in Chislehurst, Kent which is famous for its labyrinth, of course. We both got arseholed at my expense during the journey to the Giant Ashtray but I wasn't worried - my chaffeur would be waiting for me at Euston. Well it wasn't a chaffeur as such. It was a driver from Charlton Taxi Company.

Soon after joining Charlton I had struck up a deal with the

local taxi firm - on Thursdays they would pick me up at Euston and take me to my hotel. On match days they would pick me up at the hotel and take me to the Valley and after the match they would take me to Euston for the train back to civilisation. And all the drivers wanted for running me around were two tickets for the game which cost me nothing - not a bad deal all round, hey?

Anyway back to the story. I got into Euston and sure enough my cab was waiting. I got in with Janine and asked the driver if he would take her home after dropping me off at the hotel. That's exactly what happened.

The next morning I went to the Valley and noticed a police car in the car park. I thought the club had been burgled but no, the rozzers had come to arrest me.

It seems that the Delicious Janine had a fertile imagination - she had gone into a police station and accused me of raping her in the back of that taxi. I was hauled off to Charlton nick and officially charged with rape. I was then released on bail pending trial.

Of course the trial never materialised - the driver of the taxi confirmed that I had never laid so much as a finger on the lying madam. Nevertheless the story hit the local papers and it's right that mud sticks. Susan gave me a few queer looks and told me in no uncertain terms that she had taken her last taxi ride with me if that was going to happen her on the back seat.

I hated London with a vengeance and still do to this day. I had heard before hand that Londoners were cold and unfriendly, but I soon found out that this was a myth. My neighbours were the salt of the earth. It was London itself I detested. It was like a giant ashtray with lights - dirty and overcrowded. Driving was a nightmare because the roads were so congested.

The club house Sue and I were given overlooked Blackheath. The homes in that area were some of the costliest in England. Next door but one lived Eurovision winner Sandie Shaw who always took to the stage in bare feet for some reason. Two doors further down lived Manfred Mann, who fronted a rock band of the same name which was bettered in popularity only by The Beatles.

Charlton offered me two options. I could buy the house for the same price they had bought it for, or I could pay them £1 10 shillings (110p in today's money) rent and rates. Charlton had bought the house for £7,000. If I had bought it and kept it, the house today would be worth in excess of a million pounds. Know-all Hince decided he didn't want a house and elected for the rent and rates alternative. Just goes to show that I was as stupid then as I am now.

As time went on I became more and more disenchanted with Firmani in particular and London in general. Firmani always criticised but never praised. His treatment of the younger players was particularly cruel. Many times I saw one of the kids coming out of his office with tears streaming down his face. I knew Firmani hated me, but I didn't give a toss. We hardly said a word to each other from the day I joined the club.

One Sunday, shortly after my arrival, Sue looked out of the window and asked if I knew anyone who owned a blue Mercedes because one had just parked outside. Of course I knew who it was, God fearing, no drinking, no smoking Firmani. I opened the door and he was stood there.

"What do you want?" I asked.

"I've come to take you and your wife to church," he said.

"Go stuff yourself," I replied. "I've got better things to do with my day off."

That was the first of the many nails I would drive into my own coffin at Charlton. At the end of my first season at the Valley, we were taken on holiday as a reward for escaping relegation. Some reward! Some holiday!

We were actually taken to Holland, everyone's favourite holiday destination. We stayed in an old people's home which wasn't licensed to sell alcohol and if that wasn't bad enough, we were told we would be playing five matches during our stay. You must remember that this wasn't a pre-season tour to sharpen us up, this was an end of season tour after a gruelling season. The last thing we needed was more matches. We needed to recharge our batteries. Firmani had other ideas. He was a tyrant, who could make Hitler look like a childminder.

Never once were we allowed out of that hell home. All the lads had promised wives and kids that they would return with presents. Firmani was even going to deny us that. After a week in which we played two matches against Ajax and Feyenoord (we won both) tyrant Eddie said we could go out. We could either go to Amsterdam on a shopping trip or go to watch a match involving Millwall, who were also touring Holland. With a show of hands we voted to go shopping. That made no difference to Firmani, we were going to watch Millwall whether we liked it or not. According to Eddie, preferring to go shopping rather than watch a match made us a disgrace to our profession.

On the way to the match in our team bus, I hatched a plan with my great mate Moore and the hilarious Scottish striker Matt Tees.

"Listen," I said, "twat face can force us to go to the match, but he can't force us to watch it."

When we arrived at the ground, I spotted what I was looking for - a bar. And that's how we "watched" the match - getting pissed as newts in that bar. We never saw one moment of the action. Much, much later, Firmani sent in one of his flunkys to tell the merry trio that if we weren't on the bus in the next minute, it would go without us. I gave the flunky a little message to Firmani. It was short but sweet, "Fuck off".

I knew the Millwall manager, Benny Fenton, slightly, so I went into their dressing room and asked if we could get a ride to our concentration camp. He agreed but only as far as Amsterdam, which was over 20 miles from our base in the hamlet of Bloendhal. Still, it was better than nothing. We armed ourselves for the trip with as many bottles as possible. By the time we were dropped off we were even more blotto. Every time we flagged down a cab, Matt would collapse onto the street and the cabbie wouldn't take us.

In the end I hatched another cunning plot. I would flag a cab, and Moore would prop Matt up. It worked. We finally got a cabbie to take us. It must have been three in the morning and turning light when we made it back to Stalag Nine. Waiting for us at the entrance was Firmani and chairman Glickstein. Matt, in his drunken state, did what all the others had dreamed of doing – he grabbed Firmani around the neck and started to throttle him. Firmani's eyes popped out like they were on sticks. His face turned a fetching shade of black. Graham and I had no thought of rescuing the gasping Firmani, he would have died there and then if Mother Nature hadn't intervened, Matt collapsed again as the booze shut down his brain.

For that little escapade, all three of us were fined two weeks' wages. I was mortified. Not because of the money, but of what Sue's reaction would be. Well think about it. We had just spent two weeks in a country where there are more prostitutes than pigeons. You come back home and tell the missus that you have been fined two week's wages for having a drink. Will the missus buy that? No chance. She'll be thinking that you've brought disgrace to the club by being photographed doing horizontal jogging with a slapper in some sleazy brothel.

Amazingly, Sue accepted my explanation without batting an eye. Graham and Matt weren't so lucky. Mooro was walloped with a rolling pin by his better half, while Matty had a frying pan bent over his bonce...

By this time I had decided I had to get away from Charlton. The main reason of course was Firmani. He wouldn't even give me an occasional day off to enable me, Sue and first baby Nic to come back to Manchester to see our family and friends. I asked

Firmani for a transfer and – no surprise – he agreed immediately. He looked relieved to be seeing the back of someone who he felt was a troublemaker. I was similarly relieved to be turning my back on a control freak.

Believe it or not, several clubs were still interested in me. Bristol City, who had tried to sign me from City, made an offer. I don't know what the bid was but if it would have been £1.50p, Firmani would have accepted it. I turned them down and did the same to Millwall, Crystal Palace and Southampton.

Then one day the phone rang and on the other end was the Bury manager, Colin McDonald. He asked if I would like to join the Shakers. I didn't ask what my wage would be, I simply said "yes" – and another disastrous chapter in my career was about unfold.

"SHAKER" HINCE

I DIDN'T LIKE Bury. The town or the football club. The club housed us in a tiny bungalow off Brandlesholme Road, it was a dump. They should've knocked it down and built a slum. You couldn't swing a cat in the place – not that any self-respecting cat would've crossed the threshold.

I'm willing to concede that there are many friendly people in the old mill town, obviously I was unlucky. That bungalowed estate was jammed packed with miserable bastards.

One summer's day I was playing soccer with a tennis ball with a nephew. We were kicking the ball outside my own premises and do you know what one of my "neighbours" did? She called the police. Miserable old twat!

I thought the police would ignore a call like that but, oh no, it must have been quite a quiet day in Bury because the police came roaring into the avenue with the siren blazing. Obviously kicking a tennis ball in the street in Bury is a hanging offence.

Out jumped four Bury coppers. I thought they would give

me a ticking off. But no, I was hauled off to the nearest cop shop and charged with breach of the peace. Thankfully commonsense prevailed and the charge was dropped. I considered throwing a brick through that witch's window. But I decided not to as breaking a window in Bury probably carries a life sentence.

The first thing I didn't like about the Shakers was the pitch itself. After the wide open spaces of Maine Road and The Valley it was like playing on a postage stamp. Wingers - or at least this winger - detested tiny pitches. You cannot hide on them (one of my favourite pastimes once the game had started) and you couldn't lose your marker. That meant more tackles and more kicking - which went against the grain. One, I was a coward and two, I always believed that physical contact should not be allowed in the beautiful game.

I should have mentioned that I scored on my home and away debuts for City and Charlton (against Plymouth Argyle and Huddersfield respectively). Oddly enough the same thing happened at Bury - two in my home debut against Fulham and one against Derby County in my first away match for the Shakers. It suddenly dawned on me that I always score on my home and away debuts but never afterwards. Pity I didn't get transferred sixty times a season. I would have been England's top goalscorer by a country mile!

There is not much more I care to remember about my disastrous spell at Gigg Lane. I freely admit that I was to blame. I had only joined the club because I was home sick at Charlton. By this time I was planning to return to journalism and my heart wasn't in it at Gigg Lane. I played like a stump.

At the end of the season - you won't be surprised we got relegated - I re-joined *The Ashton Reporter* on a short-term basis. Instead of being posted back to the Gorton office I was sent to the Mossley branch to cover for their one and only reporter, who was on holiday. Nothing happened in Sleepy Hollow until the day when I covered the cases being heard at Mossley Magistrates

Court.

One case was hilarious. A man from Mossley had been arrested for stealing a trainer from a gym in Manchester. When police searched his flat they found thirty nine similar trainers under his bed. When the police asked him why he pinched trainers he answered "I wank into them".

When the evidence at his trial had been completed the senior Magistrate asked the trainer-wanking thief if he had anything to say before the verdict was announced. I looked about for a defendant but couldn't see anyone. Then a court official carried a chair into the dock and I understood. The villain was a dwarf. A head appeared in the dock. It was indeed a midget. I laughed out loud and received a withering look from the Magistrate.

The Magistrate then asked the tiny defendant why he had committed those weird offences. Mickey the midget looked the Magistrate straight in the eye and said, "it's because I need a fuck every 25 minutes". Now just try writing that story up in a family newspaper. I went back to the office and didn't even try. I was still too busy laughing.

It was during those summer months that the Bury supporters had their annual meeting at a huge pub not far from Gigg Lane. They had flocked there in larger-than-usual numbers because they were going to vote for the worst player in Bury's history from goalkeeper to outside-left. For most positions there were lengthy debates and heated arguments. For my position, outside-right, there was none. The assembled gathering voted unanimously that yours truly was by far the worst outside-right they had ever watched "playing" - if you pardon the word.

I read a little snippet a couple of days later in *The Bury Times*. Was I dismayed or embarrassed? Quite the reverse. I had made my mark in the history of Bury Football Club. Not a lot of players achieve that distinction, do they? I've always believed it's better to be remembered for something rather than instantly forgotten!

A couple of weeks later I took the fans' advice and told Bury that I was quitting professional football. Strangely not one official at Gigg Lane asked me to re-consider. Obviously they were as sick of me as I was of them.

Actually I wasn't quitting football as such, I had been asked by the Crewe manager Ernie Tagg if I would play for them on a part-time basis. On top of that I ran into an old mate of mine named David Duffy. He had been a major producer at ITV and had built up a tidy nest egg but Duff wanted to be his own man so he opened a press relations office in the city centre. He asked me to join him as his firm's sporting director. The salary was hugely attractive - £60 basic plus bonuses. Remember we are still in the early seventies. Some top class First Division players weren't earning that.

On top of that Ernie Tagg offered £20 a week and £15 travelling expenses to sign for Crewe. It wasn't that long before this that Johnny Haynes had made headlines by becoming England's first £100 a week footballer. I was still in my early twenties and about to sign for a lowly fourth division club and I was earning £5 less than the legendary Haynes.

For the first time ever I was minted - but it wasn't to last as you'll discover if you can bear to read on any further.

STAN BOWLES
& FOUR SHILLINGS

WORKING WITH Duff was a doddle - although I earned my salary. I was working every day for *The Manchester Evening News* as a freelance sports writer and would then go on the dreaded "dog-watch" at the *Daily Mirror* (midnight to 6am). I had to be back at the News by 8am, which didn't give me much time for sleep but that never bothered me, I was young, fit and eager in those days. Now I am old, unfit and pissed off if I have to work for ten minutes.

One day my old pal Stan Bowles walked into my office. His career had gone downhill since Maine Road - he was another Georgie Best. He had run up huge gambling bills and had gone AWOL from major matches both in England and in Europe. It came as no surprise when the Blues handed him his P45 and told him to shove off.

Stan had phoned me a few days earlier and said he had been offered a trial at Bury. He asked me if he should accept the offer and I said "no", but as usual he didn't take my advice and accepted a three month trial at Gigg Lane. I knew he would hate playing for Bury and I was right. Three months? He didn't even last three weeks.

Before one away match he kept the manager, board of directors and players waiting for hours in the Gigg Lane car-park. When he did eventually turn up in a cab he told the manager, grumpy

McDonald, that he would have to pay the taxi fare because Stanley, as usual, was broke. Bury cancelled his contract on the spot and poor Stan had to walk home in the rain.

When he came to see me in Manchester it was the same old story. He was married to Anne by this time. She had presented him with two kids (*presumably his*) and they were living in a hovel. He told me the gas and electricity had been cut off, the bailiffs had taken all the furniture and his landlord was about to evict him if he didn't pay his rent arrears pronto. I'm telling you Stanley could bring tears to a glass eye.

By now I was playing for Crewe so I phoned Ernie Tagg and asked if he would sign Stan. Obviously Taggy knew all about him, Stan's escapades were in the papers every day. I told Ernie that if he could get Stan's head right he would have a gem on his hands. Ernie told me to send him along and he'd be waiting for him at Crewe station.

"How am I going to get to Crewe?" said Stan. "I haven't got a penny to my name." I phoned Piccadilly train station and asked them the price of a one-way ticket to Crewe. The answer came back "four shillings". I rustled through the change in my pocket and gave Stan the four bob. He looked dismayed, obviously hoping for more.

"What do I do if I nod-off on the train and miss Crewe station?" he asked, "I wouldn't have the money to get back."

"Stan," I replied, "don't nod-off."

Stan didn't nod-off on the train and Ernie was waiting for him on Platform Two. Before the two had exchanged a single word Ernie had stuffed twenty pounds into Stanley's shirt pocket (remember £20 was the equivalent of hundreds by today's standards) and Stan was hooked on Crewe from that moment, signing a contract the next day. Stan and I were now team-mates for the second time.

I soon discovered that he hadn't changed one iota, he still gambled for Britain. In those days there was a betting shop opposite the main entrance at Gresty Road. Betting-mad Stan was in there like a moth to a lightbulb, he couldn't resist it. Joe Mercer, when he later became England boss, commented that if he could pass a betting shop like he could pass a ball, Stan would have been a world-beater.

It got so bad that phone calls from his wife Anne started to come into the club saying that by the time he got home on payday he would have one shilling left in his pay-packet. That bookmaker opposite Gresty Road must have thought that Stanley was a bookie's dream.

So The Alex came up with an answer to Stan's betting addiction. They gave him ten shillings out of his pay-packet and the rest was taken by odd-job man Tommy Doig to Stan's wife Anne. For a while peace resumed in the Bowles' household.

I've neglected to tell you why no player ever wanted to leave Crewe - even though the club was propping up the rest of the football pyramid. Crewe didn't just bend the rules, they drove a bus through them. When I joined them from Bury I was a free agent and not entitled to a signing-on fee under the rules which prevailed at the time.

After I had agreed to join Alex, Ernie asked me to meet him in the social club. Rules or not he paid me a signing on fee; it was £370-10s, which he took out of the till. They were the social clubs takings from the night before. At least £50 of the fee was in coins, they were so heavy that when I put them in my pocket my trousers fell down. When I went home to the newly acquired 'Hince Mansions', the missus was waiting for me. I didn't say a word. I simply threw all the notes and copper into the air. She caught the lot before they hit the carpet. Sue really was the original Careful Christian.

On the field everything I had promised Ernie about Stan came true. If he was playing today he would be worth millions. He was far too good to be playing in the lowest league in England and the scouts of bigger clubs soon began to flock to Gresty Road. In 1972 he was signed by Carlisle manager Ian MacFarlane (who we had both got to know as assistant manager at Maine Road) for the princely price of £10,000.

Stan was a sensation at Brunton Park. I once drove up to Carlisle to meet up with him and then to watch him play against Spurs in an FA Cup replay. We met up and he took me home and his wife prepared our tea. Remember this was only a couple of hours before kick-off in a very important match for both clubs. What she dished-up was a huge steak and kidney pudding, a mountain of chips and a full loaf of bread. Surely Stan couldn't gobble that meal so soon before a match. He ate the lot. We were picked up by one of Stan's team-mates "happy" Stan Ternent who went on to become a highly successful manager.

Neither Stan B nor Stan T talked about the coming game. Instead they argued about which one would perform the most 'nutmegs' during the match. Stan B said he would do 10 so Stan T said he would do 11. Both were big betting men so they each wagered £20 on themselves. I was supposed to be reporting on the match but all I was doing was counting nutmegs because I had the kitty.

By half-time Stan B had 28 to his name, Stan T's score was still on nil. The Press-Box at Brunton Park was near the touch-line and as the players walked off, Ternent walked over and said, "Stop the counting Hincey, just give the bastard the money!"

Stan was brilliant that night and due to him, "mighty" Spurs were beaten 2-0 by "minnows" Carlisle. Me and the two Stans had a night out to celebrate at a nightclub called "The Border Line". Carlisle, as I'm sure you know, is only a cock's stride from Scotland.

Don't ask me what we got up to that night because I've no idea. All I remember is waking up the next morning in Mr & Mrs Bowles' spare bed with no shoes, no shirt and a message on my chest written in lipstick which read - "Chipolata cock, you are fucking useless".

Another highlight of my time at Crewe was when I was asked to appear in a testimonial for our long serving full-back Peter Leigh against Manchester City. My wife Sue had no interest in soccer but she wanted to come to this game, if only to see what I was rewarded with for playing in the match.

Players in those testimonial games were traditionally given very expensive gifts by the player who had been granted the testimonial - solid gold pens, Rolex watches, diamond encrusted wrist-bands, so Sue's imagination ran wild with the possibilities.

Of the game itself I remember very little. I do recall that the then famous Coronation Street actress Sandra Gough was due to kick-off the match. She was, at the time, the nation's sexiest pin-up. She came into our dressing room to put on a football kit and stood there in front of us stark naked. Sexiest girl in the country? I wouldn't have shagged her with yours!

After the match, which I think Crewe won, Sue was waiting all agog in the car. I had been given a box after the match and she couldn't wait to see what I'd received. Would it be a solid gold pen or a Rolex we could've sold for hundreds?

I opened the box and lying there was... a dead chicken. Some present that was. We couldn't pawn it so we did the obvious - we had it for tea.

Anyway back to Mr Bowles who, as mentioned, had already bagged a £10,000 move to Carlisle. Manager MacFarlane was a strict disciplinarian and had more than one bust up with rebellious Stan. One day Stan threw a 'sickie' and asked Anne to phone the club to say he wouldn't be in for training.

Half an hour later there was a bang on Stan's front door. Anne opened it and stood there was the Carlisle manager wearing a face like a smacked arse.

"Where is he?" he demanded.

"In bed," Anne replied.

Without another word Ian dashed upstairs to find Stan in bed with a copy of *The Racing Post* and probably having a "hamshank" under the covers. Ian didn't say a word. He ripped back the covers and yanked him out of bed. Ian carried him to his car and threw him inside. Before Stan had recovered his wits Ian had jumped into the driver's seat and locked the doors.

He drove to Brunton Park and parked up on one of the nearby streets. In bare feet and wearing just his stained y-fronts, Stan had to walk to the club's front door past dozens of startled but amused members of the Carlisle public.

Stan trained that day, alright, but he never threw another sickie.

★   ★   ★

JUST AS HE HAD been at Crewe, Stan was too good for Carlisle - who were then in the old second division. Scouts from the big boys flocked to Brunton Park to watch Stan play and it came as no surprise when he signed for QPR who, in those days, were one of the biggest clubs in the country. Stan was bought to replace an idol at Loftus Road, Rodney Marsh who ironically signed for City, and the QPR fans quickly realised they had found another gem in our Stan.

Those fans adored him. Mind you his off-field habits hadn't changed. One day he invited team-mate Gerry Francis and his wife to dinner. There they sat at the table drinking away merrily while Anne cooked the meal. Just as they were tucking into dinner there was a hammering on the front door. Anne opened it and there stood three burly bailiffs.

Obviously Stan had not been paying his bills... again. In they marched and removed everything that wasn't nailed down: TV, chairs, table, armchairs, sofa - you name it, they took it.

Gerry told me that story himself. He was terribly embarrassed for Stan and Anne but said Stan never batted an eye-lid. He eyed the meal on the floor and said "At least the bastards haven't taken the grub!" and that's how the Bowles' and the Francis' had their dinner - sitting on the floor in a completely empty room!

Such was Stan's form at QPR that I was delighted, but not surprised, when he rang me to say that he had been selected for England.

A couple of days later I received another call, this time from the great *Daily Express* writer John Roberts. John must have known from somewhere that Stan and I were great mates. He invited me to lunch at a Greek restaurant in Manchester to discuss Stan's career which I readily accepted.

The next day a brilliant article by John was published in the *Express*. John listed all of Stan's clubs: City, Bury, Crewe, Carlisle, QPR and finally an England cap. His punch-line at the end of that article was wonderful.

"Stanley Bowles has come a long way on Hincey's four bob."

THE NEWS

THE ACCOUNTANT AT the *Manchester Evening News* obviously knew his onions. He worked out that I was earning more from the paper as a freelance than the employed reporters. It made financial sense to take me onto the staff, so that was what the *News* did. So in the summer of 1972 I became a Newsman.

In many ways I was sorry to leave Duff, who was one of the funniest men I've ever met, but I must admit that working all day as a freelance for the *News* and all night for the *Daily Mirror* was taking its toll on me. I took a drop in salary to join the *News*, but at least I would be able to see my wife and kids again.

Also, because of the long distance travelling involved, I had to leave lovely Crewe. I couldn't expect the *News* to let me have two extra days off every week because Crewe were playing on the south coast or up in Geordieland. Macclesfield Town gave me a nice option because being in the Northern Premier League in those days meant their away games were close at hand. So I accepted their offer to join the club and became a part-time Silkman.

Nothing much of consequence happened during my years at the Moss Rose other than the time I played for and reported on the same game for the *Evening News*.

I should explain that we didn't send staff writers to cover non-league matches and Macclesfield in those days were in the now defunct Northern Premier League. We only printed a six paragraph report on these matches and they were supplied by local freelance or 'stringers'.

I was due to play for Macc against Bradford Park Avenue when the local 'stringer' phoned the *News'* Sports Desk that morning to say that he had been taken ill and couldn't cover the game. The Sports Editor at the time, Vernon Addison, came up with a cunning plan. He phoned me to ask if I could cover the match I was playing in.

"Come on Hincey," said Vernon, "it's only six paragraphs, three at half-time and three at the end." So that's precisely what I did.

At half-time I used the Macc secretary's phone to send three paragraphs to the sports desk via the copy-taker and I repeated the process after the final whistle. I picked up a *Pink* that evening and if I say so myself the Macclesfield report was outstanding. Every paragraph started with the name 'Hince' - here's a sample, "Hince danced past three player before whipping over a sensational cross which was shamefully wasted by the Macclesfield centre-forward".

Every paragraph was the same. The match report suggested that I had taken on the Bradford Park Avenue team singlehandedly. Of course I neglected to name the scorers because I wasn't one of them. In fact in the entire six paragraph report the only Macc player mentioned was yours truly.

Well you've got to take the chance while you can haven't you? How many players have played in a match and then written the match report for a newspaper? I reckon Sue Barker should ask that on Question of Sport.

Needless to say, I was employed by the *News* as a sportswriter. The other soccer writers on the staff were the lovely Manchester United reporter David Meek, a rotund jovial scouser named Matt D'Arcy and a Manchester City reporter whose name is not worth mentioning as it would reduce the standards of this book to gutter level.

Matt and I were the district sports writers and we had around twenty clubs to cover. Those were the days when the *News's* circulation went as far as Liverpool, deep into Derbyshire and Yorkshire.

I loved reporting on matches. It was an adrenalin rush because they were done live. Every ten or fifteen minutes the phone would ring and you would have to ad-lib a piece back to the sports desk, via the copy room. Five minutes from the end you would add the intro and the job was done. Bang on 4.45 the presses began to roll and by 5 o'clock the *Pink* would hit the streets. Quite remarkable. Basically we only had one hour to sell the *Pink* because the newsagents shut up shop at 6pm. At its peak we were selling 300,000 Pinks in sixty minutes - even more remarkable.

Of course, because it had to be rushed off the presses, the occasional blip was printed. So in one of my match reports "ricochet" became "Rick O'Shea". In another game involving Oldham Athletic keeper Andy Goram was floored when a thunderous shot from the opposing striker hit him smack in the knackers. I was live on the phone at that moment and this is how I described the incident, "Keeper Goram was floored on 43 minutes after he was hit in the nether regions, and that led to a mad scramble for the missing ball".

All went well in my new role until one Saturday when I had an Oldham match to cover and the missus needed to get one of the locusts a birthday present.

I told her it wasn't a problem. She could drop me off at Stockport station where I would take a train to Piccadilly and from there to Mumps station in Oldham. I would make the reverse journey but at Piccadilly I would jump onto the London Express because all of them stopped at Stockport. Those trains left on the hour so I told Sue to pick me up from Stockport at precisely ten minutes past six.

Everything went as planned, at Piccadilly station I bought a single ticket to Stockport for the princely sum of two shillings and boarded the first train with 'London' on the front.

Within minutes I was waiting at the door ready for the train to pull into the platform only it didn't, it whistled straight through.

"That's odd," I thought to myself, "all the London trains stop at Stockport. This one must be stopping at Wilmslow. Susan won't be pleased. It will take me another half hour to get back."

At Wilmslow the same thing happened - straight through. Now I was really panicking. "Susan will be livid. Obviously the first stop must be at Crewe (every train stops at Crewe) but it will be eight o'clock before I get back to Stockport."

Crewe arrived and disappeared in a rattle of wheels. Now I was in big trouble with Susan. Remember there were no mobile phones in those days. There was simply no way of letting her know of the pickle I was in. I looked for someone to help and spotted two railway policemen with faces like a wet weekend.

"Excuse me," I said to one of them, "When does this train stop?" Their answer made me feel suicidal.

"When it hits the buffers at Euston."

Apparently I hadn't boarded the London to Manchester Express, I had boarded a non-stop fan's special - Arsenal had been playing at Old Trafford that day.

It was only when I returned to my seat that the full implications hit me. How was I going to get back to Manchester? All I had in the way of money was loose change.

As we neared Euston, the Brothers Grimm approached, to inform me that when the train stopped they were going to escort me to the Station Manager's Office.

What they really meant was frogmarch me. All the way up the platform they marched me. I felt like Most Wanted. People were nudging each other and whispering. They probably thought I was the Yorkshire Ripper.

I stood there before the Station Manager like a schoolboy waiting to be caned by the headmaster. I thought he would be able to help me out of my dilemma but the situation quickly deteriorated. The Station Manager asked me for proof of my identity and amazingly I didn't have anything with my name on it. No press card, no driving licence, nothing.

"I've had it now," I thought. "They're going to charge me with some sort of offence and leave me to walk back to Manchester." Then a brain-wave hit me. I would phone Susan and she would verify my identity. I asked the Station Master if I could use his phone on reversed charges and he agreed.

By this time it was almost midnight and I knew Sue would probably be asleep. My home phone rang for ages until it was answered. I heard the operator ask Sue if she would accept a reverse charge call from Euston and a sleepy voice said "From where?"

After a moment or two the operator connected Sue.

"You're never going to believe this, darling." And that was as far as I got.

"You drunken bastard!" yelled Sue and with that she slammed down the phone.

Now I was dead in the water - no valid ticket, no money and a wife (or it could now be ex-wife) who had just disowned me. The Station Master looked at my crest-fallen face and asked me what Susan had said.

"Drunken bastard," I replied.

The station master burst out laughing. "I know now you are telling the truth," he said. "Only a wife would talk to a husband like that!"

So that night, by courtesy of British Rail, I travelled on the sleeper from London to Manchester for nothing. The train didn't arrive at Piccadilly until the next morning and believe me it was a long, long walk from there to Hazel Grove but I wasn't complaining,

I had travelled 400 miles by train that day and it cost me two bob. Who says BR didn't provide value for money?

★

IN THE EARLY seventies George Best, one of the world's greatest players, shocked soccer by announcing his retirement at the ridiculously young age of 27. After a few weeks of heavy drinking and a touch of soul-searching, George had a change of heart and said he was prepared to give it another go with United.

He returned to Manchester and the *Evening News* decided to make him one of their columnists and I would act as his 'ghost'. If you are not familiar with the term I should explain that ghosted columnists don't actually write the column, they are interviewed by reporters who then write the column in the player's name.

I had known George quite well for a number of years. We were roughly the same age and had joined our respective clubs at roughly the same time. We used to meet regularly at the Plaza Dancehall on Oxford Street in the sixties, so it was logical that the *News* decided I should be George's 'ghost'.

George agreed to do the column and we quickly resumed our old friendship and within a few weeks we were both on a flight to Benfica. George had yet to play a senior match for The Reds since his second coming at Old Trafford but he had been asked to play for a World Eleven in a testimonial match for the legendary Portuguese striker Eusebio at the Stadium of Light in Benfica, United felt that playing a semi-competitive match would improve George's fitness levels, so they allowed him to fly out to Benfica and I, as his 'ghost', went with him.

George was still headline news so it was no surprise that the plane to Lisbon was packed with other journalists eager to report on George's comeback game.

On the night of the match my fellow hacks and I were taken by coach to the Stadium of Light. All the journalists picked up their passes at the press window – all that is bar yours truly as the office secretary had forgotten to order me one. I panicked but thought I'd try to bluff my way by showing my English press card; the minder on the door leading up to the press box didn't bat an eye-lid. He just waved me through.

I had already been asked by the morning paper's reporters if I could try to make my way down to the dressing area at half-time and grab a word with George. If they waited until the end to speak to him they would miss their deadlines. So that's exactly what I did – showing my press card I was waved down to the pitchside area past a couple of dozen armed guards and police.

I knocked on the World Eleven's dressing room, showed my press card and was beckoned inside. There, having a half-time cuppa, were some of the greatest players on the planet. Never underestimate the power of an English press-card.

I passed on some of George's comments to my morning paper friends and the next morning we flew back to Manchester. George, by the way, was conspicuous only by his absence that night. To say he had a stinker is an understatement.

On the Friday after my return I got a phone call from a reporter friend called Norman asking me if I was going to the Stockport County match that evening, County in those days played their matches on Friday night and I told my pal that I was going. Stockport is my local club and I had become a familiar face there, I didn't even have to show my press-card because all the doormen knew who I was and what I was doing at Edgeley Park.

At half-time Norman and I went downstairs for a cuppa and a sandwich in one of County's lounges. On the door was a real 'Jobsworth' – a weasly individual in full commissionaire gear. As I was about to go in, he stopped me. "Where's your pass?" He demanded. I told him I hadn't got one and showed him my press-card.

"You can't get in here with that," he said, "to get in here you need a pink pass at half-time and a white one at full-time."

I just cracked up, tears of laughter were rolling down my face.

Norman was bemused and asked what I was laughing at.

"Norman" I said, "a couple of days ago that press-card got me into one of the great stadiums in the world past dozens of armed police and into the World Eleven's dressing room in Lisbon's Stadium of Light. But it can't get me into Stockport County's tea room!"

The odd snag aside, I loved reporting on the various clubs and for many years I kept a notebook of the crazy things said by managers, but mostly by chairmen, who were always befuddled, senile, former millionaires who knew toss all about football.

Derby County had been relegated to the Third Division, and their doddery old chairman was asked why it had happened. "I put it down to a lack of harmonium in the dressing room" was his reply.

Another chairman sacked his manager because "He didn't smile enough". Yet another explained away his side's lowly position in the league because "We can only play in the dark".

One day I phoned the Bury manager for some team news. His star striker was called Steve Johnson. He read out his team for Saturday's game and there was no Johnson. I asked the manager why he wasn't in the line-up and his answer was priceless. "Steve is injured," said the manager, "he's strained his Hercules tendon." I suggested that the club's physio should treat the "Hercules" tendon with Ajax – but the advice fell on deaf ears.

The daddy of all dropped bollocks came from the late Manchester United chairman, Louis Edwards, who had an unfailing habit of opening his mouth and putting his foot in it. I remember going to a press conference at Old Trafford where the former Chelsea boss, Dave Sexton, was due to be introduced as the managerial successor to the sacked Tommy Docherty. Louis, Dave, Secretary Les Olive and Sir Matt Busby came in and took their seats. Louis stood up and in his spluttering manner said "Gentlemen of the press, I'm sure you will join me in welcoming to the club our new manager

- Tommy Docherty. Oh fucking hell!"

This was the time, you may remember, when crowd violence was ruining the reputation of English soccer. The Reds had witnessed some ugly scenes at Old Trafford, while Chelsea under Sexton had also had their share of idiots causing serious trouble.

One of the journalists present asked Sexton if he had any plans to deal with the troublemakers at Old Trafford. Before he had chance to speak, Chairman Louis sprang to his feet. "I beg your pardon," he lisped. "I beg your fucking pardon but I think you will agree with me that at the last two Cup finals our hooligans have been fucking superb."

On one occasion United were playing in Spain and were invited to a reception at the British Embassy. Louis seemed blithely unaware that it was Britain's Embassy in Spain and that all the officials were blue-blooded Englishmen.

Louis was introduced to the Ambassador who was educated at Oxford and was a highly decorated officer in the Second World War where he had been a major in the Queens Light Infantry. The Ambassador shook Louis' hand and said in his plumy tones, "Welcome to our little shindig, Mr. Edwards."

A look of astonishment came over Louis' face.

"Fuckin hell," he spluttered, "you speak good English."

Louis compounded his faux pas by then asking the Ambassador if he served in the war. When receiving the answer in the affirmative, Louis then dug the hole even deeper.

"Which side were you on in the war – them or us?"

The Ambassador replied that, yes indeed, he had been on England's side in the Second World War.

That must have settled Louis' mind as he walked away repeating, "It's a small world... a fucking small world..."

THE LATICS

As TIME MOVED on at the *News*, I began to concentrate more and more on Oldham Athletic. I sensed something was stirring down at Boundary Park and I was soon proved correct.

The Latics at the time were lingering in the lower reaches, and their attendances were pathetic. Before every home match, the crowd changes were announced to the team - (oh, please yourselves).

One of their former players, Jimmy Frizzell, had been appointed player-manager. I actually played against Jim during my career, the dirty little Scottish bastard. Jim and I hit it off from day one. He took me into his confidence and his dry sense of humour used to crease me up. He must have been a natural born manager because, little by little, the Latics began creeping up the table.

As an example of Jim's success, in the early seventies the Ford Motor Company introduced "The Ford Sporting League". The club who scored the most goals in a month would win £2,500. The club with the most amount of wins over the season would get the grand prize of £50,000.

The Ford people obviously believed that the publicity would stretch right across the country. Newcastle would get the money one month, Man Utd the next and maybe Spurs the next. This would ensure they would get the publicity they were seeking in the North East, North West and down South.

That masterplan never materialised because "little" Oldham dominated it. They won every monthly award and the grand prize. The only publicity Ford ever got was a few lines in the *Oldham Chronicle*. Thanks to the Latics, the Ford Sporting League lasted one season.

But the Latics were delighted. They built a new stand, and fittingly christened it the "Ford Stand" and for the first time manager Frizz had some decent cash to spend. Oldham, under Jim, raced up the Football League. Crowds increased and better players were signed. Keeper Andy Goram emerged through the club's youth system and went on to become one of Scotland's all-time greats. Although the crowds at Boundary Park were pitifully thin, both Jim and I firmly believed that a place in the First Division was within the team's grasp. Then one day during the close season the bombshell dropped. Oldham announced that they had sacked Jimmy Frizzell.

I phoned Frizz and asked him to meet me in his local. When we met up I asked him why he had been sacked. Jim, who was as honest as the day is long, said he hadn't the foggiest. He had been summoned to the Chairman's office, where he was told that the board fancied a change. A few weeks later the Oldham Chairman Harry Wilde - a clown in the wrong sense of the word - called a press conference to explain his actions. I've already told you that chairmen are fond of uttering stupid statements. Harry's statement of why he had sacked Frizz took the biscuit.

"I accept that over the years Jimmy Frizzell has performed miracles for this club," said Harry, "but now I am looking for another manager to do better."

I never thought Oldham would find a better manager than Frizz. I was wrong. Waiting in the wings was the former Everton, City and England striker Joe Royle. If I thought that Jimmy Frizz had built a good side at Boundary Park, then I hadn't seen anything yet.

Joe had finished his playing career at Norwich because of a persistent back injury. He had no managerial experience when he applied for the Oldham job and he was worse than second hand by the time the Latics got him. In fact he fell off the back of a lorry! It's true. Joe was driving up from Norwich for his interview when his car broke down on the motorway. He flagged down the next vehicle and arrived at Boundary Park sat in the back of a lorry.

With Joe and me it wasn't the usual manager/reporter

relationship, where the manager is economical with the truth and the reporter takes no notice and writes what he wants anyway. Joe and I became close personal friends, and I'm delighted to say the friendship has endured to this day.

When he was Oldham's manager I would phone him early on Sunday morning before writing my match report for the following day's paper. Joe's wife, Janet, was and still is, a stunner. One Sunday morning I phoned Joe early and said I hoped I wasn't disturbing him. He had already nicknamed me Weasel.

"No Weasel," he answered. "I am just lying in bed with a film star who has the biggest tits in Britain."

"You in bed with a film star?" I sneered, "with your looks it must be Lassie." That joke is still running to this day. Now when he picks up the phone I ask how Lassie is. His answer is always the same, "Well I've given her two Bob Martins, and her nose is nice and cold."

In the nineties, of course, Joe took the Latics into the top flight. I had been covering them for the *News* but I never got to see them in the Premiership. At the end of Oldham's promotion season, the *Evening News* Editor, Mike Unger, asked me to come to his office. He said he was getting shut of the City reporter, a sentiment I heartily agreed with, and that from now on I was the *Evening News* Manchester City correspondent.

As you already know I've been a blue all my life. Watching God's Own Club, and being paid to do it, was a dream come true.

But I had also grown very fond of Oldham Athletic. I had reported on their rise all the way from the depths of the fourth division into the Premier League and I desperately wanted to report their top-flight games. In desperation, I said to the Editor that I would be both the City and Oldham correspondent.

"So you can report two different matches at the same time, can you?" said Mike, "don't be daft; you're our City man from now on."

LIFE WITH THE EVENING BLUES

S O LIFE BEGAN as the *Manchester Evening News* City correspondent and for the best part of the next fifteen years I lived on Cloud Nine. Peter Reid had just been appointed manager and Sam Ellis was his assistant. I quickly got to know and like both of them and they seemed to like me. If a manager doesn't trust his local reporter, the job is virtually impossible to do properly. My first task as the City man was a real ball-breaker, a pre-season tour to sunny Italy with all expenses paid.

Going on tour is the best and quickest way to get to know the players. I soon discovered for instance, that goal-keeper Tony Coton had a strange sense of humour. As we stood on the runway at Manchester Airport waiting to embark I noticed "TC" visibly shudder. I asked him what was wrong and he replied in a grave voice "Hincey, do you see that wall at the far end of the runway? I've just had a vision that we crashed in to it on take off and burst into flames." I nearly went home there and then.

Most players had seen the light about smoking by then and had quit the habit but oddly Keith Curle hadn't. I say "oddly" because centre-half Curly was the quickest player I had ever seen. But Curly had an odd way of smoking because he never bought a packet of fags. He smoked other people's. He came up to my seat as we levelled off and asked me for a cigarette. Now I would never begrudge anyone a fag so I handed him my packet of Dunhill. Big mistake! There were eleven cigarettes in that packet and Curly helped himself to ten of them.

We stayed at a magnificent golf hotel high up in the Dolomites and the view was spectacular. It didn't seem blisteringly hot because of the thin air but within a couple of days I looked like a beetroot.

The tour itself I thought was ridiculously hard on the players. If I remember right they played ten games in eleven days. I remember thinking that they wouldn't be fit for the start of the season, they would be knackered. Finally after the last match, the players were allowed out on the town. Several of them asked me to come along but I had already agreed to have a meal and a few slurps in the hotel with Peter and I'm glad I did.

The next morning the players staggered down for breakfast looking half-dead. Big Niall Quinn had a gash above his eye and scouser Steve McMahon had a black eye. Slowly the tales of the player's escapades began to emerge. The lads had visited every bar in the village and had smashed up the last one. One "playful" City player had pushed new signing Rick Holden through a plate glass window; how he escaped without a scratch I'll never know. He could have been killed.

Quinny and Macca, who were great mates, decided to have a fight outside what was left of the bar. They only stopped when armed carabinieri turned up and threatened to throw both of them in the pokey.

As the tales were unfolding, we could hear sirens in the distance. Then 8 or 9 police cars roared up to the hotel's front door. With them was the proprietor of the smashed bar who had, understandably, made an official complaint. The players were given a choice, fork out for the damage or you're off to the cooler. The players forked out alright. Soon there was thousands of Lire on the table. Probably about £4.10p in our money but the proprietor seemed satisfied and the first crisis of Peter's career was averted.

I sat next to Peter on the way to the airport and promised

him that he wouldn't read a line about last night's ructions in the *News*.

"What ructions?" He said. "That was just a typical Liverpool night out!"

I knew there and then that I was going to enjoy my new job.

★   ★   ★

PETER REID CAME agonisingly close to building a championship winning team at Maine Road. There were a few dodgy signings of foreign players no-one had heard of accompanied by mysterious brown envelopes but by and large the majority of his signings were smack on. He didn't dither when it came to spending the chairman's money and within a matter of weeks defenders Keith Curle and Terry Phelan had been drafted in from Wimbledon.

Chairman Peter Swales was heartily disliked by the City supporters and for the life of me I couldn't understand why. True, he was a self publicist. The joke doing the rounds was that Peter wore an engraved medallion around his neck bearing the words "In case of accident call a press conference". But I had no doubt in my mind that he was City through and through.

Alongside the signings of Curle and Phelan (both costing £2.5m) City also had the costliest keeper in the country (Tony Colon) as well as the two costliest defenders. And it was chairman Swales who begged, borrowed or stole the money to bring that trio of quality players to Maine Road. The City fans should have been cheering him on on match days instead of booing him.

Listing a catalogue of matches under Peter is as boring as hell, so I'm not going to do that. All I will say is that in his first season and a half the blues were always in the top six. A succession of serious injuries to key players caused a dip in performance over the second half of his second season in charge but there was never any danger of the side being relegated and Peter settled down for the long haul at Maine Road.

He certainly didn't see the sack coming - and neither did I. the axe fell four games into his third season as manager. Four games! What a ridiculous time to sack a manager.

Swales did a peculiar thing after Peter's departure. He decided he wanted nothing to do with decision-making at Maine Road (as if!) and appointed as Chief Executive John Maddock, a friend of mine who had previously been the Sports Editor of *The Sunday People*.

John knew everything about journalism but fuck all about football. Within days of his appointment the players were up in arms. John claimed there was "disharmony" in the dressing room. There was because a "know-nothing" was suddenly their boss.

John's remit was to find a manager to replace Peter and he played the situation for maximum effect. He teased me and the other hacks that were monitoring the situation at Maine Road.

"The new manager will blow your socks off," he said, "he's the greatest manager in the world."

Like everyone else, I wondered who the mystery man could be. Terry Venables? Glenn Hoddle? Graham Taylor? What was clear was that my blessed Blues were going to get the best in the business.

Early one morning John phoned me in the office. He had identified City's new manager. Again he played cat and mouse with me. "I left Bramhall at eight this morning, and for the last three hours I've been travelling south," he said. I was perplexed. He's travelling towards London but who has he cherry-picked as the new manager?

Then came a match at Maine Road against a team I can't recall. After the match Maddock came into the press room. I ordered him out. It was his club but rules are rules. I would have needed a pass to enter the inner sanctum of the boardroom. This was my territory. I told him that he came in by invitation only.

Fifteen minutes later he phoned me on my mobile and asked if he could address the press. He told me that I wouldn't regret it - he was just going to unveil the greatest manager on the planet.

Of course I relented and within a few minutes John tapped politely on the door of the press room. I opened it and invited him, and his mysterious companion, to enter. John addressed the liverish hacks and introduced his new managerial appointment - the legendary Brian Horton.

I knew all about "Nobby". His reputation throughout soccer was second to none. Nothing spectacular, you understand: captain of Luton Town and Brighton and a natural leader of men. The job he had done at Oxford United was mind blowing.

The criminal Robert Maxwell owned the club. Maxwell, owner of the *Daily Mirror*, had decided that his employers' pensions should be his pocket money. When he mysteriously 'disappeared' from his £10m yacht there were lots of conspiracy theories. Was it suicide or murder? To this day I'm convinced that Maxwell is still alive and chuckling about the hundreds of old folk whose pensions he stole.

Maxwell's son, Kevin, had been given a gift by his criminal father - Oxford United. When Mark Lawrenson heard of Maxwell senior's apparent demise he did the obvious thing, he quit as manager at Oxford Utd and advised his assistant, Horton, to do the same thing. Nobby, being Nobby, dug in his heels and refused to go. He didn't have two pennies to rub together as Oxford boss but walking away from a crisis was not in his vocabulary.

So he stayed at Oxford and without a pot to piss in he somehow managed to take them into a higher league. He should have been named manager of the century for that feat.

Of course I knew all this before Maddock introduced Brian to Her Majesty's Press. Other journalists that night weren't so knowledgeable. One lad from the Press Association, who looked about fifteen to me, asked a question which, unfortunately, will live with Brian forever.

"Brian," he asked. "Who are you?"

And that provoked the inevitable headlines in the following morning papers. "BRIAN WHO?" they all said.

Nobby was - and is - a wonderful human being. If there's a bad word to say about anyone he won't be the one to say it. Much is made of the relationship between managers and journalists. All I can say is that Nobby was a dream to work with. As honest as the day is long and the original good egg. I love him to bits - no, not in that way! But his job at Maine Road was doomed from the start.

City were quite literally unmanageable. Chairman Swales had decided that he no longer wanted anything to do with the club, and all the decisions would be taken by Maddocks. What a cop-out that was.

Off the pitch the natives were getting restless. The atmosphere inside Maine Road was positively poisonous. The fans didn't watch the games. They turned their backs to the pitch and hollered "Swales Out" for the entire ninety minutes. In the end the fans got their way. Peter Swales stood down, allowing Francis "Barney Rubble" Lee to take control at Maine Road.

Joe Royle phoned me the moment he heard the news and told me that City had just acquired the first Chairman/Manager in the history of English football. Big Joe was smack on the ball. The Francis I knew and liked in the sixties bore no resemblance to the Francis of the early nineties. He had become a control freak who knew fuck all about modern football.

I remember having a chat with the superb Paul Walsh at the Platt Lane training complex, shortly after Lee's takeover.

"Walsh," snapped Lee, "come to my office because I want to speak to you."

Paul tutted and said in a voice Lee must have heard, "I'll have to go, Hincey. The fat controller wishes to speak to me."

I knew then that Walsh's career at City was effectively over. Within a few days he was back at Portsmouth in exchange for Gerry Creaney, who was the worst player ever to represent the

Blues since myself.

Like his predecessor Peter Reid, Nobby came agonisingly close to building something good at Maine Road. He bought the German striker Uwe Rossler who quickly became a cult figure with the Maine Road faithful. Uwe was a gentleman on and off the pitch. Years after leaving City he phoned me to say that he had lung cancer - even though he never smoked. Experts say that you don't recover from lung cancer. I'm happy to tell you that Uwe is the exception to the rule. He's made a full recovery, which is the least I expected from one of football's good guys.

There was no end to Brian's torture under Lee's tenure. Win, lose or draw Nobby never missed an after-match press conference. But all that changed after a match against Wimbledon at Selhurst Park (the Dons were ground-sharing with Crystal Palace at the time). At the press conference Nobby was conspicuous by his absence. The blood suckers from Fleet Street decided that he'd been handed his P45 by the repugnant Lee.

The following morning Brian phoned me to explain his absence. The Blues had played exceptionally well against the Dons, and were desperately unfortunate to go down 2-1 but know-nothing Chairman Lee knew better, of course. After the match he had kicked down the City dressing room door and bollocked Nobby in front of his team. Inexcusable! I knew then that Nobby's days were numbered.

Brian wasn't sacked - he sacked himself. He was at an end of season manager's meeting in Bounemouth when he read in a morning paper Lee was about to get rid of him. Brian left his fellow managers and drove north to confront Lee at his mansion in Wilmslow.

Brian wasted no time with small talk. He simply told Lee to "back me or sack me". Lee, to his eternal shame, picked the latter. And the Blues had lost their best manager since the days of the legendary Joe Mercer, way back in the sixties. To make matters worse, Lee decided to strip the club of its assets. Within a matter of weeks he had sold Coton, Phelan, Curle and striker Niall Quinn. Later he was to flog the wonderful Gary Flitcroft. Lee had ripped the heart out of the team. But he phoned me and ordered me to congratulate him in print for reducing City's wage bill.

I told him to go away in jerky movements - cheeky twat!

★

IN TIME, FRANCIS Lee's reputation spread through the soccer grapevine. Joe Royle was right - no manager worth his salt would want a job where the tail is wagging the dog. After dangling various tasty morsels to the press Chairman Lee offered the vacant manager's post to his old pal Alan Ball.

Alan had been a wonderful player for Everton and Arsenal, in fact despite Geoff Hurst's Hat-Trick I still believe that he was Man of the Match when England beat Germany in the '66 World Cup final. But as a manager, Bally was shit.

He took the Blues down in 1996 and I'll never forget the final game of the season against Liverpool at Maine Rd. The Blues needed to beat the scousers to secure their top-flight place. With seconds to go the score was 2-2 and relegation beckoned. City midfielder Stevie Lomas had the ball by the corner flag. Alan screamed at him to play for time - seemingly un-aware that a draw would send his team through the trap door. Stevie did as he was told and City were relegated.

That match took place on a Sunday. My day off was the Monday but Alan asked me if I would meet him the following morning at the Platt Lane training complex. I still remember everything about that meeting. I was there at 9 o'clock but Bally was late. He said he'd had a dentist appointment, as a coach he'd probably had his teeth taken out and a row of seats fitted.

His first words took me aback. "I'm glad we've been relegated., he said. "This gives me a chance to clear the drains." Have you ever heard a manager say that he was happy that his side was relegated? No, me neither.

Alan told me that his "clear the drains" policy would mean 26 players would be dispensed with. It goes without saying that this was major news and I lost no time in reporting the interview to the *Evening News*.

Later in the day Bally's interfering wife phoned me in the office. She wanted to give me a bollocking for the article but I was having none of it.

"Where's Alan?" I asked to which she replied "Still at Platt Lane." I phoned him and said that his wife had just attempted to give me a bollocking. He replied that I deserved it.

"Wait a minute," I said, "I only reported what you told me this morning."

"No I didn't," squeaked Alan, "you've made up that story."

To every question I got a "NO."

No, I hadn't spoken to him a couple of hours earlier.

No, he hadn't said he was about to "clear the drains". How can a reporter work with a manager like that?

Ball's disastrous reign ended in defeat at Stoke. Of course he blamed me. In the after-match press conference he said that City were unmanageable because of that "Low-Life over there." I turned around to see who he was pointing at and realized it was me. Funny that, I don't remember playing in Bally's side that season!

He also named me in an interview on Sky TV, where he again called me a "Low-Life". The following day I went to Lords to watch the mighty Lancashire demolish Essex in a knock-out final. All the lads in the press box had heard Bally's accusations aimed at me the night before.

Peter Johnson, of *The Times*, suggested that I should sue Alan for defamation of character. Then another journalist piped up, "Hincey, could you stand there in court under oath and swear you're not a Low-Life?"

I declined to sue.

★

AFTER THE FALL of Ball City went through a revolving door policy that saw three managers appointed in as many months during the latter part of 1996. The experience of Ball's successor, Steve Coppell, summed up Lee's reign.

The former Manchester United and England winger fell for Lee's patter and became City's new manager but lasted just thirty days at Maine Road. There was much nasty speculation in the newspapers about Coppell's departure. AIDS was one suggested reason, child abuse another.

To be honest I went for AIDS. The Coppell I saw after thirty days in charge at Maine Road bore no resemblance to the Coppell I had interviewed on day one of his tenure. When he announced his departure he was gaunt and ashen-faced. All of the symptoms of that dreadful disease.

What I discovered later was that Steve didn't have a deadly disease. He had simply made the wrong decision when accepting the offer to manager City and he was man enough to admit it.

THE THREE LIONS

OVER THE YEARS, my stock had grown at the *Evening News*. In the mid-nineties I became the paper's Chief Sports Writer, which was a great honour. Never in the paper's history have they had a Chief Sports writer, and they haven't had another one since I retired.

I was given another title at the same time - the paper's England correspondent. That meant I would report on England's matches, wherever they played in the world. At least I was going to clock up some air miles.

Not that I clocked up many on my first England trip - it was a World Cup qualifier against Northern Ireland. The team flew out from London. I flew out from Manchester with my old friend Sammy McIlroy, who was going to summarise the match for Irish television.

We couldn't believe it when we saw our 'exclusive' jet on the tarmac. It looked as though it was falling to bits. It had an outside toilet and elastic bands wrapped around the wings. We climbed aboard and there were only four seats. Sammy and I were the only passengers, which wasn't surprising seeing the state of the thing. God must have still been a lad when that scrap heap with wings was built.

Amidst a great deal of clattering and banging, the plane eventually managed to get airborne and we wobbled off towards Belfast. There was no cockpit. The pilot just sat in front of us, with a few controls before him. Sammy, who didn't like flying at the best of times, convinced himself that the pilot was pissed.

After about half-an-hour the pilot turned around and asked us to look down to the left. He said we were flying over the Isle of Man. We looked down and there it was. Fifteen or so minutes later, Sammy looked down to the left again and his eyes popped out. He told me to look down too. I did, and there was the Isle of Man again!

"I told you the driver was pissed," whispered Sammy, "he's lost his way; we're going round in fucking circles now. We won't get out of this alive because he'll run out of petrol sooner or later."

By some fluke we managed to reach the Irish coast and began our descent to Belfast Airport. When we got over the runway the plane dropped like a stone, hit the runway, and bounced back up about a hundred feet. At the second landing attempt, we only bounced up seventy feet. The third attempt only forty feet, and so on and so on until the plane came to a rest. Naturally enough, Sammy and I didn't come back in that plane for the return trip home. We came back by boat!

The "troubles" were still raging the next time I returned to

Belfast for an International. Staying in the same hotel as me was a young news reporter from *The Daily Mirror* called Steve. He told me that all *Mirror* reporters were required to do a stint in Belfast. It was a dangerous place to be in while the war with the IRA was taking place. Even as Steve and I talked we could hear the distant rumbling of bombs going off.

Steve had only been in Belfast a week and already his nerves were shattered. On his first day in *The Mirror* offices in Belfast, the place had been blown to bits by an IRA bomb and he was lucky to survive. Two days later a roof sniper had taken a pot shot at him, and blown away the toe cap of his shoe. He decided to do all his work from the hotel after that but that had been targeted two days before I arrived. I wondered why half the windows were missing.

Steve told me that he'd had enough. *The Mirror* had told him that he'd be sacked if he didn't complete his tour but Steve couldn't care less. He said that being on the dole was better than being dead. He was going home that night. Steve rang me the next day to say that on the flight home a bomb on the plane had gone off but somehow no-one was injured. Three bombings and one toe cap blown off in the space of a week. I've never made my mind up whether he was the luckiest or unluckiest man on the planet.

The troubles in Northern Ireland escalated and there was massive security when the FA chartered jet landed at an airport outside Belfast. Our coach had an armed escort all the way to Belfast and the hotel we were due to have lunch at had been completely cleared - and this was the security for the journalists. God knows what the security must have been like for the England team.

During the flight we had all been given a box which contained six miniature bottles of alcohol: Gin, Rum, Brandy, Whisky, Vodka and Cointreau. At lunch I suggested that we had a whip-round for the lads who were guarding us and all the journalists agreed. So I asked one of the waitresses for a carrier bag, and everyone put in two miniatures. It was a good haul. There were sixty or seventy journalists on that trip.

I took the bag outside and saw a sergeant standing there. I asked him if his lads could have the booze and he said that of course they could and I could pop the bag in a Land Rover parked near-by. I walked over to the Land Rover - pulled open the covers at the back - and found myself staring down the barrel of a rifle, being held by a young trooper. What a foolish thing to have done. Just as well that young soldier didn't shoot first and asked questions later.

★

WHEN I TOOK over the role of England Correspondent for the *Evening News*, the national manager was Terry Venables. Yes he was a bit of a cockney rascal, a real wheeler and dealer but there was something likeable about 'Tel Boy'.

He seemed to treat every day as a good day, he always had a smile on his face and he had the press eating out of his hand. More than anything he knew more about football than I will ever learn if I live to be one hundred and fifty.

He came agonisingly close to steering England to success in Euro 96 at Wembley and, to my mind, it was a scandal that he was dismissed by the FA for non-football reasons.

His successor was Glenn Hoddle, who I could never take to. It struck me that if he was made of chocolate Glenn would lick himself to death. Hoddle was a bit spooky as well, he even bought a 'Mystic Meg' type called Eileen Drewery along who he claimed could sort out a player's mental problems.

That eerie lady had individual sessions with all of Hoddle's players. When little Dennis Wise went in she sat him down and asked him what he wanted. "A short back and sides please" chirped Dennis who never appeared again in a Hoddle squad.

When the FA finally handed Hoddle his P45, again, oddly enough, for a non-football matter, Kevin Keegan took charge of the national side and this was one man I was eager to meet.

I flew out with the other journalists to Spa in Belgium for Euro 2000 and we stayed in a magnificent hotel only a stone's throw from the England Headquarters. Over the next two weeks I got to know Keegan fairly well and I was tremendously impressed by him.

He gave a press conference every day in the late afternoon but for the evening paper reporters they were a waste of time. We had already passed our deadlines so anything Keegan said would appear first in the morning papers. So I approached the FA's press officer David Davies (an old friend of mine) and asked him if Keegan would agree to hold a second daily press conference just for the evening paper lads.

To my surprise Keegan agreed and he was simply wonderful – he would speak about Alan Shearer to John Gibson from the *Newcastle Chronicle*, he would give his opinions on the London players to Michael Hart of the *Evening Standard* and I would receive the benefit of a few words on the Manchester based players for the *News*. The evening paper bunch were extremely grateful to him for making our jobs so much easier.

Living for a fortnight with the Fleet Street Jackals was an experience, but then again dying is an experience and I wouldn't reccommend that either. Those morning paper hacks have egos the size of Blackpool Tower. They don't report news, they try to make the news themselves. They have no respect for people who know more about football than they do and they are invariably vicious and vindictive.

Many times in that hotel in Spa, I heard them talking amongst themselves. It was clear to me that they were waiting for one of the Neville brothers to make a costly mistake so they could rip him to pieces. When Phil Neville conceeded the penalty which sent England out of Euro 2000, my heart sank. I knew what was coming for him in the morning papers the following day and I wasn't wrong.

Poor Phil was slaughtered by the London 'rat pack'. Yes, his clumsy tackle dumped England out of Euro 2000 but not one London-based reporter mentioned that throughout the tournament he had been England's most consistent player - by a country mile.

Before I covered Euro 2000 I always believed Alex Ferguson was being paranoid in claiming that the London-based media had an anti-Manchester agenda. Two weeks in Spa with the 'gutter' press from the giant ashtray convinced me that Sir Taggart was spot on all along. I can only put that down to one thing - green-eyed jealousy at what Alex and his teams have acheived down the years.

Keegan was still the England manager when the qualification matches for the 2002 World Cup got underway, but not for long. England's campaign began disastrously and a 1-0 defeat against Germany at Wembley was the straw that broke the camel's back. Keegan resigned 15 minutes after that match had finished and I was at his press conference an hour or so later when he announced he had thrown in the towel.

I had mixed emotions when I wrote up that story. He looked on the point of tears when he announced his resignation and my heart went out to him because he was clearly deeply hurt after being booed off the pitch by the England supporters that night. But Keegan had been in the game long enough to know that being abused by supporters goes with the territory for both players and manager.

Christ, I was booed by my own supporters at every club I played for! The Charlton fans at the Valley would call for me to be taken off during the pre-match kickabout! The one thing you need as a manager or a player is a thick skin. It seems that Keegan's is about as thick as tissue paper.

For the next qualifying match in Finland the FA drafted in its technical director, Howard Wilkinson. My heart sunk when I heard the news. Down the years I had a number of run-ins with 'Wilko' during his days at Leeds United. It's fair to say that he hated me with a vengeance and the feeling was reciprocated.

One reason for my dislike of him was his attitude. Wilkinson always struck me as being a smart-arse. Once he held a press conference when, as a virtual unknown, he was appointed Sheffield Wednesday manager. One of the reporters asked him if it was true that he once been a school teacher. Wilkinson nodded.

"What did you teach, Mr Wilkinson?"

"Children," deadpanned the new Owls boss.

See what I mean about being a smart-arse. Just as well he never became City boss - I would have topped myself.

Anyway back to Helsinki. Wilko's press conference the day before the match against the Finns was unusual in that we were all given the England line-up for the next day's game, whereas normally the media are given the teams an hour before kick-off. I glanced down the team-sheet and noticed that Michael Owen's name was missing - at the time Owen was arguably the world's most prolific striker.

I stood up and asked if Owen was injured. Had we been the only two people in the room he would probably have told me to fuck off but in front of hundreds of journalists from England and abroad he had no choice but to answer the question.

"No", he said, "Owen is not injured".

"So you've dropped him then because he played in the last match against Germany"

Wilkinson's response to that was a beauty. "How could I drop him when I didn't pick the side against Germany". You can't argue with logic like that. Thank God he only managed England for that one match!

Of course it wasn't long before Keegan was back in club management and as much as I was annoyed and distressed by the sacking of Joe Royle by City, I was looking to renew my working relationship with his successor.

Only 24 hours after his appointment I drove down to City's

training complex in Carrington to interview Willie Donachie. As I parked up I spotted Keegan being handed his sponsored car only a few yards away. I walked over and offered him my hand with the intention of welcoming him to the club and wishing him every success. I didn't get the chance - he saw me and bolted back into the offices.

I couldn't understand why a man who had been so friendly and helpful throughout Euro 2000 could react like that but sadly I soon came to realise that Keegan, the England manager bore no resemblance to Keegan, the City boss. The personal battering he had taken from the tabloid press in Euro 2000 had affected him deeply. I tried to explain to him that there had not been a word of criticism of him during the tournament in the *Manchester Evening News* but those words fell on deaf ears.

In Keegan's mind, every sporting journalist was the son of Sam. Behind even the simplest enquiry Keegan felt there was a grenade waiting to go off. I found him almost impossible to interview during his time with the Blues. To this day I believe him to be a good and compassionate man but I also believe that his track record proves that he is just not cut out for the cut-throat world of football management.

Of course the manager who replaced Keegan in the England hot-seat couldn't have been more of a contrast. Sven had skin the thickness of Rhino hide and he needed to have as time and again the media (particularly the Jackals) set him up for a fall. He must have driven them bananas because no matter how they tried they couldn't break down the barrier he had erected between himself and his critics.

If Sven didn't want to answer a compromising question he would just sit there with a silly smile on his face. If he did respond to a question the answer was always the same.

"We did very vell, Gerrard did very vell. Beckham did very vell." To be honest with you Sven's press conferences as England manager were a waste of space. The FA's press officer at the time was former BBC man Paul Newman who I had know for years.

When Sven's nocturnal habits were making front page news, I asked Paul why Sven always managed to look so calm and relaxed when other managers in the same situation would have been falling to pieces.

"That's easy," replied Paul, "he simply doesn't give a shit what people think or write about him."

What a great attribute I thought. An England manager who doesn't give a shit - it's a pity that Keegan didn't have Eriksson's mental strength, we might have won the World Cup if he had.

★

As PART OF my duties as the Chief Sportswriter on the *MEN* I wrote a weekly column based around sport which the readers seemed to enjoy. But I quickly discovered that expressing an opinion can be hazardous and extremely costly.

One week I had read that the Leeds United manager, Howard 'dullard' Wilkinson was in line to become England's new manager. With a name like that he should have been razor sharp (get it... oh suit yourselves) but I had always found him to be as dull as ditchwater. So in my next column I wrote that if Wilkinson became England manager I would stop reporting on football and switch to netball - nothing wrong with that is there?

Oh yes, there was - at least as far as Wilkinson was concerned. He threatened to sue me for libel but in the end settled for a public apology which I refused to write - our lawyer did it.

I saw him in press conferences for three years after that, whenever City met Leeds (no he didn't get the England job, thank God) and he never said a word to me. Then after one match against the Blues at Elland Road he had obviously eaten someone who disagreed with him and he asked me to make myself known.

I stepped forward with a smile on my face and offered my

hand. He ignored it and embarked on a tirade which went on for a full ten minutes. His face turned brick red and the veins in his neck looked like they were about to explode. My face was covered with his spit (most unhygenic) and I couldn't understand a word he was saying. Well it's difficult to make a sentence out of "fuck, fuck, fuck, fuck...".

But I did make sense of his Grand Finale. He said I was married to a "Fat ugly bitch who stunk like a pig". True enough, I thought, but how the fuck did he find out? You don't think he'd been sleeping with the missus do you?

My next tangle with the laws of libel involved Karren Brady who had just been appointed as Birmingham City's Chief Executive. Physically Karren was (and still is) a very beautiful woman but she has the sense of humour of a dead sheep. In her column for a local paper in Birmingham she complained that she had been refused admission to the Blackpool boardroom at half-time.

The article was picked up and carried by the nationals and Karren was interviewed on TV - everyone agreed she had been treated dreadfully. Everyone that is except yours truly - I have always believed that there was a place for women in football but that nobody had yet got round to digging the hole.

At Blackpool, as at most clubs, the boardroom is men-only and has been since the year dot. Now Brady was trying to change tradition and in print I called her a 'bimbo'. Big Mistake. The shit hit the fan again.

Our Assistant Editor - a little Jock named Jimmy Ross - came running down to the Sports Desk waving the writ. He looked like Neville Chamberlain proclaiming "Peace in Our Time".

"Hincey" hissed Jim, "show me the offending article!"

I produced it and within seconds he was shouting "Bimbo, bimbo!" Now with growing rage, "you cannae call her a fucking bimbo. All your articles are supposed to be vetted. Who vetted this one?"

MEMORIES...

When I told him that he had vetted it himself his demeanour changed, he paused for a second before walking away muttering, "the woman has got no fucking sense of humour".

However that wasn't the end of the Brady story. Our lawyers decided that the word 'bimbo' had libelled her and we paid her £16,000 out of court. Again Jimmy came running down the office waving his piece of paper.

"£16,000," he screamed, "you've just cost us sixteen fucking thousand pounds, you nincompoop."

"Only £16,000" I laughed, "That's a third division pay-out. Take it out of my expenses!"

Jimmy was not amused.

Another litigious reader of my columns was Ken Bates - he's made millions out of suing for libel. That must be Ken's motto "If it's breathing, sue it". He was Chelsea chairman at the time and I was at Stamford Bridge to watch them play the Blues. As I walked into the Main Reception area Master Bates was having a furious row with the City chairman Francis Lee. Bates was effing and blinding in front of women and children and I didn't like it.

In my next column I launched into Bates. I wrote of his confrontation with Lee and called him "The angriest man in Great Britain" along with any other insult I could think of. In due course another writ arrived but this time it was heavy duty. The case was to be heard at the High Court in London.

We hired a top barrister to run the defence and the night before the case was to be heard he phoned me, he had a right plummy voice.

"Mr Hince," he minced, "I have your article before me. Is Mr Bates really the angriest man in England?

"I don't know," I replied.

"Mr Hince, does Mr Bates really bellow like a bull with toothache?"

"I don't know," I repeated, adding "well bulls must get toothache sometimes but I've never heard one bellowing."

"Mr Hince," continued m'learned friend, "did Mr Bates really try to fry the Chelsea fans to a frazzle as you point out in your column?"

"Not really, but he wanted to electrify the perimeter fences at Stamford Bridge to stop the crowd getting onto the pitch".

"Mr Hince," said the barrister in grave tones, "we haven't got a facking leg to stand on - we are going to settle out of court."

Do you know what the settlement figure was for Ken Bates? £93,000! Add that to the settlement figure for Karen Brady and I had cost the *Evening News* £109,000 in libel damages.

Mind you it was worth it to see Jimmy's face when the letter arrived - a delicate shade of black with just a trace of steam emanating from both ears.

SIR TAGGART

I'VE OFTEN BEEN asked what makes Sir Alexander Ferguson tick. Well if I knew the answer to that I'd be a top Premiership manager rather than an old scribbler scratching around for a living.

I've known the United manager from the first day he walked into Old Trafford all those years ago. We aren't pally-pally but I know him better than most and I am here to tell you that he is nothing like his public image.

Sure, he's got a temper, which of us hasn't? But beneath that fiery exterior lies a warm, compassionate nature. He doesn't suffer fools gladly and down the years he's not been slow to remind me when I've done something to upset him.

The season after The Reds ended their 26-year wait for the championship title I pestered him for an interview. After much badgering he finally agreed - with one proviso, I had to be in the car park at the training ground when he arrived or there would be no interview.

In those days United trained at The Cliff in Broughton, Salford. I live in the Garden Village of Hazel Grove in Cheshire. Normally it would take me no more than 45 minutes to drive to the Cliff but this time I was taking no chances. I left home at 6am. There was no traffic on the roads at that time barring the odd milk float and a few drink drivers and I arrived at the Cliff at 6.30.

It was still pitch black and guess who was waiting for me? Yes, you're right, the fiery one with a beaming grin on his face, the bastard!

Of course he had set me up but he didn't cancel the interview. Instead he made me a cup of tea and a bacon sandwich and I spent a pleasant hour in his company. The interview was purposely bland, I didn't want to ruffle Alex's feathers, it was merely a review of how the season had progressed so far and his expectations for the remainder of the campaign. At one point I asked him how he would react if United won the European Cup as he would have the full set by then. Would he retire?

Alex said he wouldn't but with every trophy in the bag he would become less of a hands-on manager and delegate some of his duties. The interview was published and when I saw the headline my blood ran cold. It read "Fergie set to retire". I knew I was in trouble because Alex had said no such thing but all managers believe the reporter also writes the headlines.

The next morning the telephone on my desk jangled and I knew who would be on the other end. You must understand the ramifications of that misleading headline, United were then a public company and because of that headline the club's share price had slumped on the stock exchange costing the Reds millions of pounds.

No doubt Fergie had been bollocked by his chairman and now he was out for revenge. You've probably heard of Fergie's hairdryer blasts which can singe your eyebrows from twenty paces, well that's what I got when I picked up the phone. The earpiece started to melt and furious Fergie ended his tirade with "and never phone me again… for a long time".

A fortnight later our United correspondent had a day off and I had to telephone Alex.

"Oh it's you," he hissed when he picked up the phone, "I thought I told you not to phone me for a long time."

"But it's been a long time," I spluttered.

"No it's not," he replied, "it's been two weeks and two days. Anyway what can I do for you?"

Can you see the significance in that? He could remember his blast at me to the minute. He's got the memory of an elephant. What an asset for a manager. He can take one look at an opposing player and remember everything about his game months later. He must know the strengths and weaknesses of every player in the Premiership, just one example of what makes him the greatest manager of all time.

Of course United won the Champions League a few seasons later and I was fortunate enough to watch that amazing game from the press box at the Nou Camp. Quite by accident I bumped into Alex in the car park after the match and offered my hand in congratulation. He didn't accept it. Instead he gave me the kind of hug which any respectable grizzly bear would have been proud before adding "But you're still barred from Old Trafford!".

I interviewed that great United servant Brian McClair ahead of his testimonial match and he said that if any player had a problem – whether soccer related or domestic - Fergie was the one they turned to for help and advice and he never let them down.

Well in 2000 I had a giant problem on my hands - how to live without my wife Sue who passed away after a long illness. I spoke to Alex shortly after Sue's death and it was a long, long conversation. What he said will remain confidential but his words gave me the strength to carry on – that showed me the man's compassionate side.

★

I HAVE TO take the credit for dubbing Alex 'Taggart' after the Scottish detective and that moniker seems to have stuck. Can't you make up a name for yourselves - you plagiaristic bastards! But I was in a quandry after Fergie received his knighthood... calling him 'Taggart' in print seemed a touch disrespectful due to his elevation.

So at the first opportunity I asked him how I should refer to him from then on. Fergie reflected for a moment and then replied "Hincey, you may now call me Sir Taggart".

Compassionate and funny.

On the back of this book there is a picture of Alex Ferguson so I had better explain the circumstances. I attended his press conference at the Carrington Moss Complex one Friday afternoon. The following day my blessed blues were in action against Fergie's United in the derby. Just as I was leaving the room Alex handed me a mysterious looking brown envelope. His instructions were equally mysterious.

"Don't open this envelope until you go to bed and pin the contents to the wall behind you!"

I did as Fergie asked and, remember, this is the night before the derby. Inside the envelope, as you can see, is a picture of Fergie with the words "Sweet dreams, Hincey, all the best Alex".

What he was hoping for, of course, was that I'd have a nightmare instead of a sweet dream as I pictured a 10-0 win for the Reds against God's Own Team!

In the event we won that particular derby and if I had had any guts I would have returned the picture to Sir Alex along with a few choice words on the Reds ineptitude. But as a former chicken-hearted winger I opted not to.

So that's the legendary manager of Manchester United. He's a contradiction in terms; short-tempered one day, warm the next.

Will the 2008 double be Fergie's last triumph? Not by a long chalk in my opinion. He's mellowed over the years but he remains a driven man. Despite a minor problem with his heart a couple of years ago he's still as fit as the proverbial butcher's dog.

So, congratulations Alex! You've done it again. And I hope I'm around long enough to see you emulate this year's triumphs with many more to come - don't give it all up too soon Sir Taggart, you're a long time retired!

★

IN MY EVENING NEWS columns down the years I've often mentioned another great Scotsman, the wonderfully gifted former Liverpool striker Kenny Dalglish.

But all the stories about Dalglish were figments of my fertile imagination. I used to write that I was his most trusted advisor when in truth I've never met him in my life.

Kenny was managing Blackburn Rovers at the time and I would regularly write a story of him pitching up at Hince Mansions in his Robin reliant with the lovely Marina (his wife) by his side.

The Dalglishs would tuck into Sue's famous salad butties, down a couple of pints of Davenport's and then drive down to Stockport for a night at Mecca Bingo. Kenny once won £5 and refused to share it with me - well he is Scottish, remember.

Of course it was all ridiculous nonsense but the readers seemed to like it and some even believed it. I was in my local newsagents one day when one of my neighbours walked in. He was a successful businessman but clearly wasn't the sharpest tool in the box.

"Paul," he said, "I wonder if you could do me a favour. You know my son David is a fanatical football fan, the next time Dalglish visits could you get his autograph for my lad".

I was gob-smacked, I had more chance of getting laid by Halle Berry than getting Dalglish's autograph but I said I would see what

I could do.

How could my neighbour think my made-up talks about Kenny and his wife were fact rather than fiction?

There's nowt stranger than folk, is there?

There is a codicil to my invented stories about the Dalglishs.

I've been friends with Tommy Docherty for as long as I can remember and one night he phoned. He told me had been to Ewood Park that day to record an interview with Kenny for the BBC. Tommy was surprised that along with the *Lancashire Evening Telegraph* there were copies of the *Manchester Evening News* strewn about Dalglish's office. When the interview had finished Dalglish poured Tommy a drink and then asked if he knew an *Evening News* sport reporter by the name of Paul Hince.

The Doc confirmed that he knew me and Kenny asked him what I was like.

"A right little bastard," came Tom's flattering reply.

What he asked The Doc next made my blood run cold. "He asked me to find out when you were next at Ewood Park."

I was taken aback, "Why the hell would he want to know that?"

"I've no idea Hincey, but I can tell you one thing, you won't be getting a glass of scotch and a fuckin' garribaldi biscuit in his office once he claps eyes on you!"

In the light of that conversation I decided it would be best to stop making up these fantasies about the Dalglishs and find someone else to mock.

LS LOWRY

AS A RESULT of my long association with Manchester City both as a former player and the club's MEN correspondent, I am often asked to speak at various branches of the Manchester City Supporters Club. One evening I was the guest speaker at the Swinton branch and was interested to discover that the meeting was being held only a throw-in away from the birthplace of the world famous painter LS Lowry.

I entertained the Swinton branch to the best of my ability and was rewarded with a Lowry Print which I have on my wall to this day. A few days later my mum Margaret popped in to see me and spotted the print and she proceeded to tell me a story which left me uncertain whether to laugh or cry.

In the early fifties mum was a waitress in the cafe of a posh department store on St Ann's Square in town. Lowry at the time was employed by his father collecting rent from shops and stores in Salford and Manchester. As an artist he was a complete unknown.

Every Monday he would pop into mum's cafe for a cup of tea and a couple of slices of toast while he was going about his rounds. Over the weeks and months Lowry and mum became firm friends. They had two interests in common: betting and football. Mother gambled all her adult life and she was particularly clever at picking winners from the horseracing world.

Every week Lowry and mum would have a threepenny bet on the results and final scores of the matches involving United and City. Invariably they cancelled each other out but one Saturday mum got everything right: results and scores while Lowry got everything wrong.

The following Monday morning when Lowry sat down in the cafe she pounced and demanded her winnings. Lowry looked crestfallen. He explained that he was stony broke and suggested a double-or-quits bet for the following Saturday to which mum agreed. That Saturday dawned and the same thing happened again. Mother swept the board, now Lowry owed her the princely sum of sixpence.

The same scenario unfolded the following Monday morning. Mum demanded her tanner and Lowry confessed to still being skint. So he tried a different way to discharge his debt. From his suitcase he took out a large pad on which he had been drawing various scenes from the locality and offered my mother three pictures as payment for the debt.

My mother, bless her cotton socks, was too clever to fall for that. She took one look at the strange match-stick figures in the pictures and turned down Lowry's offer. In fact she told him that she had a six year-old son (me) who could draw better than that!

Days before mum told me this tale, the PFA had purchased a Lowry original for £900,000. Mum could have had three originals for sixpence...

We've always been a lucky family!

COLUMNS

FOR REASONS WHICH I've never fathomed some of you have been mildly interested in my columns in the Evening Blues down the years. So here in this chapter is a random selection (in no particular order) of the sort of drivel which has been infuriating you down the years.

Mixed in with them is the occasional response of my reader. He lives in Gorton and drives around on a moped with a sign on the back which reads "Hince is an ignorant cunt".

★

This one will need no explanation unless you've never heard of Becks. If that's the case you must have been living on Mars these past 15 years.

A HEART OF GOLD

MY admiration for David Beckham reached a new level at Old Trafford last Saturday and it had absolutely nothing to do with his ability to land the ball on a sixpence from 50 yards away. In fact it had nothing to do with football at all.

For my abiding memory of Saturday's World Cup qualifier against Greece won't be Beckham's amazing last-gasp goal which took us the Japan, but the way the England captain looked after that incredibly brave little tot Kirsty Howard.

I had a lump in my throat from the moment Beckham slowly led his team out of the tunnel hand-in-hand with terminally ill

Kirsty, who has helped raise over £1m for a children's hospice despite undergoing 11 heart operations already in her short life.

The walk from tunnel to half-way line was agonisingly slow. Six-year-old Kirsty, linked to an oxygen tank, looked incredibly small and fragile amongst all those professional footballers. She looked like a good gust of wind would knock her off her feet, but that was never going to happen with Beckham at her side.

I couldn't take my eyes off the strapping England captain and the tiny little girl whose hand he was holding so gently. And the next few minutes made me weep. Right through the national anthems, Beckham's hands never left Kirsty's shoulders. He wouldn't allow the team photos to go ahead until he had once again positioned Kirsty by his side. His very last act before the game began was to stoop down and lovingly kiss his little companion goodbye.

Beckham, I am positive, was reminding himself at that moment that the welfare of one frail six-year-old girl was a hundred times – a thousand times – more important than the result of any football match.

As a dad myself, I've got a fair idea what else Beckham was thinking in those few moments leading up to kick-off time. He was thinking of his own bouncing baby son Brooklyn looking on from one of the executive boxes. He was thanking God that his own son had been born healthy and there will have been a twinge of guilt mixed in there too as he looked down at little Kirsty. If you are a parent with healthy children you will know exactly what I mean by that.

Sure, I know what some of you might be thinking. It was just another photo opportunity for Beckham. Another chance to show the country what an all-right guy he is. Rubbish. David Beckham needs publicity like you or I need a third ear-hole.

Beckham cared about little Kirsty Howard at Old Trafford last Saturday. Cared deeply. Every little tender gesture told you so. I don't know what heights David Beckham will reach in his soccer career - and I don't particulary care. But what he showed to me on Saturday was that, as a dad and as a human being, he's world class.

Dear Mr Hince,

I just wish to write a few lines in appreciation of the column you wrote regarding David Beckham with Kirsty, the little 'mascot' for the England/ Greece match at Old Trafford last Saturday. Many people I have met since were deeply affected by the joy and courage of this little girl and very moved by your most sincere article.

I work at Francis House and Kirsty is indeed a most wonderful child and totally unspoiled by all the special attention she has received. Everyone watching was very touched by Beckham's care and tenderness towards Kirsty - and the man who pushed the oxygen cylinder was also so careful and attentive.

Kirsty is typical of all the children we care for - their courage is such an inspiration, and their parents and brothers and sisters equally so.

Thank you for bringing out such a human side to the mighty world of football. It was all the more notable because, as you pointed out, Beckham had to switch immediately into focussed action with his team.

I know you are a fervent City supporter - well, we can't all be perfect! - but it is really good to see City on the up and so positive.

There's a lot to be proud of in Manchester!

Yours sincerely,

Sister Austin.

*

Dear Paul,

For a blue - you are a good fellow as well. Your write-up summed up my feelings being there at the time - and your article moved me to tears.

From one dad to another, keep well,

Yours

Stewart Kerry

*

MEMORIES...

23rd October 2001

Dear Sir,

I wrote to you personally on the 10th October last complimenting you on the "A Heart of Gold" feature which appeared in the MEn on the 9th October.

In view of you failing to acknowledge my letter one can only assume your time would be better spent working in the City sewers - you would feel at home there - that is certainly where you belong,

Your

Norman Cocker

Denton, Manchester

★

MAINE ROAD - END OF AN ERA

These columns are devoted to my beloved Maine Road. The old lady deserved a glowing accolade when her doors were slammed shut for the last time. One way or another my life has revolved around Maine Road and I hope the following columns give you some idea of how much I loved the old ground which I miss to this day.

SPECIAL WHIFF OF NOSTALGIA

WAS it my over-developed nostalgic streak at work or was there something extra special in the air at Maine Road on Saturday?

No, I've not forgotten it was a derby and I haven't been celebrating City's famous victory THAT much.

Of course the noise level gets cranked up a few notches when Blue and Red abuse each other across the sterile zone.

But I've been at derby matches before. Dozens of 'em down the years at both grounds. And I can never recall anything which matched the atmosphere inside Maine Road on Saturday. It made the hair on the back of my neck stand up.

I don't know for sure what made that atmosphere so special. But I know what I hope it was.

I hope that, like me, the City fans who sang and cheered themselves hoarse viewed Saturday's derby as the day they started to say goodbye to Maine Road.

I have to come clean here and admit that I'm hopelessly sentimental. I can use up a box of tissues watching Animal Hospital. And I was close to tears at Maine Road on Saturday.

Not so much from the joy of the result - although that was enough in itself - but from the sadness which came with the realisation that this was the last time I was going to watch a Manchester derby in the ground I have loved with a passion for the best part of 50 years.

This is the ground where, as a kid in the fifties, I dreamed my dreams, cried my tears and danced for joy from my very own spot on the Kippax.

This is the ground where I cheered my heroes, never imagining that one day, for one brief glorious moment, I would dine with kings as a Manchester City player myself.

This is the ground where I spent most of my working days as this newspaper's City correspondent. Apart from family, Maine Road, it seems, has been the only other constant theme running through my life for as long as I can remember.

Some clever dick will probably write in and tell me it is impossible to love an inanimate object. He'll be wasting the cost of a postage stamp.

I love Maine Road with a vengeance and for me the grieving process that she won't be with us much longer started at Saturday's derby as I suspect it did for thousands of other City fans.

A good hour before the start of the match I sat in the Press box and looked around my second home. The memories came flooding back in waves, especially of the great players who have graced this turf in derby matches.

Of course many I have only read about. Billy Meredith, Sam Cowan, Eric Brook, Matt Busby (as a City player). The legendary goalkeeper Frank Swift. The players I worshipped as a kid. Bert Trautmann, Roy Paul, Ken Barnes, Dave Ewing, Roy Clarke, Joe Hayes. I could name them all.

Through the eyes of a ten-year-old they were heroes, every last one of 'em simply because they wore the sky blue shirt.

In my mind I fast-forwarded a couple of decades. Tony Book, Colin Bell, Francis Lee, Mike Summerbee, George Best, Bobby Charlton, Denis Law and a hundred others all fighting their corner for their club and their supporters in a Manchester derby at Maine Road.

Somehow, as I sat alone with my thoughts on Saturday I couldn't come to terms with the fact that the next generation of stars representing the blue and red halves of this great city will be battling for derby honours in another stadium, in another place.

But then I took another look around the ground where I grew up and have spent so much of my working life. Isn't it strange that when you know you are about to lose something - or someone - your senses become more acute. You notice things that you've never noticed before.

Well, perhaps you did notice them but you didn't care to see them. I sat there looking down on a stadium beginning to fill up and it dawned on me that, as much as I love every nut and bolt in the place, Maine Road has become the house that Jack built.

A veritable dog's dinner of a ground. None of the stands match each other. There is no symmetry about the place. No clean lines.

From the air Maine Road must look like a badly-fitting jigsaw. The two uncovered "Gene Kelly" sections squeezed in at either end of the Kippax where the fans have no choice but to go 'Singing in the Rain'. They look like scaffolding with seats.

On Saturday as I watched and waited for the two teams to emerge it brought a lump to my throat to accept the fact that the old girl who I have adored these past 50 years is past her prime.

It's almost time to leave her behind and move on to better and newer things - to take that step into the 21st century which Manchester City needs to do to have a viable future.

I know all that and I accept all that. But for me watching the last ever Manchester derby at Maine Road was like closing a chapter in my life.

I know now that it won't be long before I am saying goodbye to a beloved old friend for the last time.

Yes, I know it's the right thing to do. But it won't stop me weeping buckets when that dreaded day does comes.

THE END OF A LOVE AFFAIR

THE shrinks will tell you that it is impossible to love an inanimate object. You know the sort of thing they say. You can be proud of your new car but you can't exactly love it.

Sure, your lawn-mower is a handsome beast. But love it? Now you're being silly.

Well, I don't care what it says in the shrinks' manual. Because I'm here to tell them - and you - that I love Maine Road with a passion right down to the last brick and rusty rivet.

Apart from family, that glorious mish-mash in Moss Side of odd stands, wonky seats and stone-age turnstiles, has been the one constant theme which has run through my life - and I am now nearer to 60 than 50.

And if I dare to go to Manchester City's very last match in their old home in a month's time, I can guarantee without fear of contradiction that I will be in floods of tears when the doors of Maine Road are banged shut behind me for the final time.

Personal memories of Maine Road. Blimey, where do I start?

This isn't a fleeting infatuation, you know.

This is a love affair stretching back over 50 years. How do you condense half-a-century into one article?

Perhaps that's the best place to start... 50 years ago when I was an eight-year-old just starting to learn about life and soccer in the Gorton area of this city. Even then, of course, I was a Manchester City fan. So were all my mates. Gorton, in those days, was a hotbed of City support.

If we had spotted a Reds fan on our patch we would have chased him down Hyde Road all the way into Denton. Money was tight, but that didn't seem to matter much.

All the families in Gorton in the early fifties were pretty much in the same boat.

They didn't have much but what they had, they shared.

There certainly wasn't enough spare cash left at the end of the week to treat the kids to the admission price for a Manchester City match. But that didn't matter much to us either. Because we knew how to get into Maine Road on match days for free.

So on Saturdays, when the Blues were at home, me and my pals would set off at three o'clock to walk to Maine Road.

Down Hyde Road we would march heading in the direction of the Belle Vue zoo complex before turning left to follow the old 53 bus route down Kirkhamshulme Lane and into Rusholme. Skip across Wilmslow Road and we were almost there.

By this time it wasn't just me and a few pals heading towards Maine Road. There were scores of kids - sometimes hundreds - all heading for the citadel.

Because what I knew - and what every young City supporter who couldn't afford the admission price also knew - was that at three quarter time the big steel doors of the Kippax stand would be flung open to let the early-leavers out and let the kids outside in... free of charge.

At about twenty-past four in every home match at Maine Road, hundreds of kids - me included - would pour in through those open doors into the Kippax.

It must have been an extraordinary sight. Great waves of small children being tenderly handed down above the heads of the adult supporters in that huge standing enclosure. The supporters at the front of the Kippax would shuffle back a few paces to create a crush-free zone for the tiny gatecrashers and that's how I watched my first Manchester City matches. An uninterrupted view from a ringside position - and it didn't cost me a penny.

The Kippax was still my preferred watching location when I entered my early teens and could afford the admission price out of the cash I earned from my milk and paper rounds.

I was a bit of a one-boy cottage industry in those days. The strange thing was that even though the Kippax was a standing enclosure, everyone had their own particular spot.

I have heard regulars asking an occasional visitor to edge sideways a couple of feet because he was standing in HIS place!

My place was over a tunnel in the left-hand corner of the Kippax. The same fans were there every match.

The immaculately turned out middle-aged lady from Prestwich who always provided me with a cup of steaming hot bovril at half-time. The fella in the cloth cap who worked at Metrovicks who always shared his spam sandwiches with me.

I used to wish he would develop a liking for cheese or corned beef – but he never did. Just spam.

The City players I watched at Maine Road in the 50s were my heroes... every last one of them. We probably had some duck-eggs if the truth were known but in my eyes, they were all stars.

Bert Trautmann, the finest goalkeeper I have ever seen. Big Dave Ewing at centre half who nobody got past in one piece. Ken Barnes the best half-back never to play for England. Roy Clarke, Don Revie, Bobby Johnstone and my favourite of them all... the little goalscoring machine Joe Hayes.

Of course what I could never have imagined as the 50s turned into the 60s was that the fans I stood with every other week watching City from our private bit of the Kippax would be watching me in a few years' time playing in the famous sky blue shirt.

Just how the Blues came to make the ghastly blunder of adding me to their playing staff is another story for another time. But for a couple of years as a City player I walked with kings and began to regard Maine Road as my second home. I had worshipped there and now I worked there.

I made my first-team debut at Maine Road against West Brom and somehow scored twice in a minute. I could count my good games on the fingers of one hand. And all of them were played at Maine Road.

I genuinely believe I had an affinity with the old stadium. It was as if she sensed that I loved her and she was looking after me in return.

You might think that is stupid, but I'm telling you that I never felt as comfortable or as content at any time in my career as I did when playing at Maine Road. The old girl even had a smell all of her own. It wasn't unpleasant - quite the reverse. It was almost intoxicating.

I would smell that unique smell every morning when I walked through the doors to report for training. I don't know what it was - but it was there in the air. A faint trace of liniment mixed with dubbin and furniture polish, perhaps.

That was getting on for 40 years ago. And to this day I can still close my eyes in a quiet moment at the end of the day and bring back the smell of Maine Road.

And I know, in doing so, that I'll sleep easy.

I thought the love-affair was over when I left Manchester City to join Charlton Athletic in the late 60s. I should have known better.

No more than four years later the old girl embraced me again... not as a player this time but as a sports writer for the *Manchester Evening News*.

How many times have I walked through that Press entrance at Maine Road over the past 30-odd years? I couldn't even begin to tell you. If I had a pound for every visit I could have retired years ago, that's for sure.

There was a time in the very early 90s, when I was this newspaper's City reporter, when I seemed to spend more time at Maine Road than I did at home.

I worked there, I ate there, I drank there and, on a couple of occasions, I slept there. And I never, ever lost the feeling that the old girl was glad to see me.

Now the sands of time have caught up with Maine Road - just

as they have caught up with me.

When I walk away from my beloved old stadium for the last time in May, a little piece of me will die.

Sure, I may live to become proud of City's wonderful new stadium in east Manchester. But love it as I have loved Maine Road for the past 50 years? No, I don't think so.

I've got too many memories, too much of my life is wrapped up in that particular building in Moss Side to have any room left in my heart for another.

FAREWELL TO AN OLD FRIEND

IT was every bit as gut-wrenching to be at Maine Road yesterday afternoon as I feared it would be.

And I didn't need reminding by a score of fans that I'd promised I wouldn't be there to witness the Last Rites being read over Manchester City's headquarters.

Believe me, it wasn't by choice.

Kevin Keegan has urged us not to wallow in the past but to look forward to the future that awaits us and our club in the wonderful City of Manchester Stadium. And he's right to do so.

It's time for us to move on. But I've got fifty years of memories invested in that bits-and-pieces, lovely old stadium in Moss Side – and so have thousands of City fans like me who are no longer in their first flush of youth.

And I'm sure I am speaking for every last one of them when I say that being at Maine Road yesterday was like attending the funeral of an old and dearly-loved friend.

It's the little things that get to you on an occasion like this, isn't it? The memories just flood back when you least expect them and suddenly you've got a lump the size of a golf-ball in your throat.

Just parking up in that playground at the little school facing the back of the Kippax. How can that possibly be emotional? It was for me yesterday. How long have I been using that spot? More years than I care to remember. And never again am I going to drive through those iron gates and get the thumbs-up from the girl who always waves me through with a beam on her face.

I'll miss her almost as much as I'll miss the old stadium itself.

The walk from that playground to the Press door at the far end of the Main Stand. How many times have I made that walk down the years? I've no idea but I wish I had a pound for each one.

Passing the spot on the corner opposite the ticket office where the old groundsman Stan Gibson lived. Stan loved Maine Road like it was one of his own kids. When I was masquerading as a City player back in the late sixties, Stan used to blame me for any ruts down the right-hand side of his beloved pitch. He used to tell me those ruts were caused by my nose. He was joking – I think.

I paused for just a second as I passed where Stan once lived. He would have hated this day. Apart from family, Maine Road was Stan's life. The thought of the proud old girl being bull-dozed into rubble would have been unbearable to him, I'm sure of that.

Minutes later I was looking down on the best pitch in the Premiership from the Press box right at the back of the main stand.

I can't see the numbers quite so clearly any more from so far away, age has crept up on me. The parade of legends is just beginning and now the memories are overwhelming me. Some of the stars of the fifties are taking a bow.

The very first City team I supported while still at primary school in Gorton. Roy Clarke, Johnny Hart, Roy Little, Paddy Fagan. All of them heroes of my youth. And spindly-legged Ken Barnes – Peter's dad – the best half-back never to win an England cap.

The fifties gave way to the sixties and it was time to say our thank-yous to members of the best City team in my lifetime which won so much under Joe Mercer and Malcom Allison. Tommy

Booth, such a cultured centre-half, the indomitable Alan Oakes and "Barney Rubble" himself - the barrel-chested goalscorer supreme Francis Lee, all made an appearance on the pitch.

Could I really have played and trained with those great stars for a while at Maine Road in the sixties? It seems now like it was a dream, but it's true. So how come none of them look a day older while I look like I'm ready for the knackers yard?

Kick-off time approached. The legends of the past gave way to the City and Southampton teams which would contest the last ever match played at Maine Road.

Why, I wondered, were the teams lining-up on the pitch just in front of the player's tunnel? Moments later I knew as the players were introduced to three extra-special guests as a fitting and poignant end to the pre-match build-up on this extra-special day.

Out of that tunnel stepped Nora Mercer, the still sprightly widow of the greatest manager in City history. But Joe was more - much more - than that to me. A kinder, more compassionate man never drew breath.

Behind Joe's widow strode Colin Bell, surely the most complete player ever to appear at Maine Road. What a reception "Nijinsky" received from the Blue Mooners yesterday. No surprise in that. City fans know a true world-class player when they see one.

And then, last, there was Malcolm Allison, the coach who master-minded the success of the 1968 championship winning team.

The tears welled up in my eyes as I looked down on him. So frail, so unsure in movement as he battles illness. In my mind's eye I don't see Malcolm like that.

I remember him in his prime while I was a hopeful young footballer at Maine Road in the sixties.

So fit, so strong, so handsome. You should have seen the beautiful women who flocked to his side. Big Mal had to beat them off with a stick.

There was a football match at Maine Road yesterday, but I couldn't see it.

Never in fifty years of support for the Blues have I been less interested in the result of one of my team's games. The occasion and the memories it evoked of the cathedral I had worshipped in for as long as I can remember were simply too powerful.

Bert Trautmann, Roy Paul, scoring twice in a minute on my City debut, Colin Bell's comeback game, Paul Lake's injury, Gio Kinkladze, the dignity of Brian Horton, the humour of Joe Royle.

A million memories stored away which flooded back in great waves yesterday. And there was one final memory to take to my grave in the warmth and genuine love which the Maine Road fans expressed for Shaun Goater in his final match for the Blues. Only in this stadium, only with those fans and only for that player could you witness pure emotion being expressed of that intensity.

Two hours after watching a match I had forgotten already I drove out of that school playground for the very last time. I took one last lingering look at the Kippax.

Overhead were dark storm clouds but the Kippax itself was bathed in sunlight. I know she's become a dog's dinner of a stadium in her later years, but at that moment, through misty eyes, Maine Road looked achingly beautiful.

I didn't want to be there yesterday but I'm glad I went. Had I not I would never have forgiven myself for not paying my last respects to what has been my second home for the last half century.

So goodnight and goodbye old friend. I'll never forget you.

★

RUGBY WORLD CUP

I know fuck all about rugby union. But like the rest of the country I was transfixed by England's dramatic victory over Australia in the World Cup Final of 2003. Even my traitorous grandson Connor caught the RU bug as you will read in the column I wrote to mark that glorious event.

OUR CONVERSION

EARLY on Saturday afternoon, around half-an-hour after THAT match had ended, I had a phone call from my daughter Lorren. She wanted to pass on a request to grandad from her eight-year-old son Connor.

To make sense of what I'm about to say, I have to tell you first that Connor is soccer-mad.

What I refuse to commit to print is the name of the club he supports but you've probably guessed it by now, anyway. The little traitor. Lorren had phoned to tell me what Connor wanted above all else as a Christmas present.

No, it wasn't a signed picture of a certain Scottish manager who eats kids for breakfast.

What Connor wants me to get him for Christmas is an England rugby union shirt.

And nothing I have seen or heard this past 48 hours illustrates the real significance of England's wonderful victory in Sydney better than that Christmas request from my eight-year-old grandson.

You see I'm willing to bet that today there are a million kids like Connor in homes up and down this country. Kids who, thanks to Martin Johnson, Jason Robinson and an extraordinary young man called Jonny with ice in his reins, have suddenly discovered rugby union.

England did more - much, much more than win the World Cup on Australian soil.

The real, long-lasting achievement which skipper Johnson and his magnificent team pulled off during their World Cup campaign was to take their sport onto an entirely different level.

Let's be honest. What was your perception of rugby union before the World Cup Finals began?

Let me tell you what mine was and see if you agree. It was a sport which enjoyed a degree of popularity in the Home Counties played by university graduates who trample each other into the mud and then all get smashed together afterwards in the club-house bar to the accompaniment of bawdy songs.

And that just shows what a blinkered clot I've been all these years. Because rugby union is none of the above. What the World Cup in Australia has shown me is that rugby union is a sport to match any in the world played by superb athletes whose dedication, courage and sheer bloody-minded determination puts many of their higher-paid soccer counterparts to shame.

After Saturday, sport in this country will never quite be the same again. We are not just a soccer and cricket nation any more.

In just a few weeks, rugby union has stitched itself into the fabric of this country. It has become one of this country's headline making sports and it is here to stay.

Now, thanks to England's monumental victory in Sydney our kids have got new heroes to look up to.

And not the flawed heroes of the soccer pitch who will accept the riches and the fame but not the responsibility which goes with it.

I'm talking here about real heroes who give their all on the pitch and are a credit to their sport off it.

Yes, I know we've all gone overboard about Jonny Wilkinson this past couple of days. A knighthood around the corner, guaranteed Sports Personality of the Year.

If he ran for Prime Minister right now, Tony Blair wouldn't stand a chance. But all that means little to me.

Much more important in my eyes is that there isn't a dad in this country who wouldn't welcome that lad into his family.

And how many soccer stars could you say that about?

What the World Cup has shown is that there is something noble and soul-lifting in rugby union which seems to have seeped out of professional soccer.

But I've been gripped, absorbed and excited by the efforts of Clive Woodward's men.

I won't try to kid you that I have any depth of knowledge about rugby union. What I know about the finer points of the sport could be written on the back of a stamp.

I can still remember virtually every kick in the 1966 World Cup soccer final between England and West Germany at Wembley. But you know what it's like when you're a teenager. You take things for granted.

The enormity of England's victory that day passed me by. Whoever said that youth is wasted on the young knew what he was talking about.

But this World Cup final was different. When you reach an age where you've got more life behind you than in front of you, it suddenly dawns on you that you might never again see an England team in a World Cup final. Believe me, it's a sobering thought.

I watched the final in a mixture of terror and heart-pumping excitement. If you had told me that I could work myself up into that state over a game of rugby union I would have laughed you out of the room.

But that is what Martin Johnson, Jonny Wilkinson, Jason Robinson, Will Greenwood and their remarkable team-mates have done to me during campaign in Australia.

They have dragged me and others like me from one end of this country to the other into THEIR world. They opened our eyes to the splendour honesty of THEIR sport.

And if you don't believe me ask grandson Connor and all the

others from Sunderland to Southampton are praying that they find an England shirt with the name 'Wilkinson' on the back under the tree when they come downstairs on Christmas Day. As for myself, I've already received my perfect Christ,as present. It was beamed into my front room all the way from Sydney. And I'm happy to share it with you. For the first time in over 30 years in this job I can type out "England - Champions of the World."

And you've no idea how much I've longed to write those few words. Jonny, Jason. God bless you and everyone of your team-mates.

There is none so blind as he who can not see but I can see clearly enough. Look to your laurels all you over-paid soccer stars. There is another sport vying for the attention of the paying public. And just right now that other sport is winning hands down.

Who said the good guys never win anything? Jason Robinson is a wonderful, warm and friendly man. He is also a committed Christian who wouldn't say boo to a goose.

He also happens to be one of the world's greatest Rugby union players and it was a privelege to interview him after he had played such a huge part in England's World Cup success in 2003.

*

TIME OF MY LIFE

Jason reflects on 'unforgettable' march to glory.

AT first glance he looked like most people's idea of a successful professional sportsman. Good looking, bulging muscles and positively radiating good health. But there was something different about this particular sportsman, the gleaming new World Cup winner's medal around his neck.

There's a name on that medal. And that name is Jason Robinson.

Was I really in one of the banqueting suites at Sale Sharks' Edgeley Park headquarters having an intimate conversation with THE Jason Robinson?

Wasn't it only last Saturday morning that I was jumping up and down like a deranged banshee in front of my TV when Robinson flew over the line to score that historic try in England's victory over Australia? To me a try in rugby equals a goal in soccer. And in my lifetime, before last Saturday only two men had scored a goal for England in a World Cup final - Geoff Hurst and Martin Peters in the 1966 Wembley triumph over West Germany.

Now I was sitting inches away from the third Englishman to achieve that feat.

To say I was in awe of Jason Robinson when we met yesterday afternoon is the understatement of the decade.

Believe me, even in this job you don't have a cosy chat with a genuine, 24-carat national hero every day of the week. But if he is a national hero after his exploits in Australia - and there's no "if" about it - you would never guess so from talking to him.

There's an air of modesty and calmness about him that belies his achievements Down Under and the instant fame which has engulfed him and his team-mates since that never-to-be-forgotten final. It's Boy's Own stuff really isn't it? But there again Robinson's life could have come straight out of a kid's comic as his "Billy Whizz" nickname did.

His tearaway days as a youngster with Wigan Warriors where praise and criticism showered down in equal measure.

His conversion to the union code and the reawakening of the Christian beliefs which he insists saved his career and quite possibly his very sanity. And now a World Cup winner's medal. No, you wouldn't read that even in a kid's comic.

But it happened all right. And the proof was sitting right next to me wearing the medal that he's probably not taken off since last Saturday.

"Don't be fooled by outward appearances," grins Robinson. "What happened to me and my England team-mates out there in Australia is something we will remember and cherish for the rest of our lives.

"We all had to make a lot of sacrifices to come back with that trophy. It only dawned on me the other day that I haven't played for Sale Sharks since last May. That is how long our preparation took to make sure we got it right. The entire World Cup finals were an unforgettable experience but the final itself eclipsed anything I could possibly have imagined.

"We had some limited feedback about how the people back home were responding to our campaign in Australia. We knew that for once, rugby union had pushed soccer off the back pages and we felt good about that because all of the England players like to feel that we are ambassadors for our sport.

"But coming out of that tunnel for the final really blew our minds away. All those England fans in the stadium. We couldn't believe so many had travelled so far to support us.

"Of course I still re-live the try I scored in my mind. I can still picture Lawrence Dallaglio making the break and giving the ball to Jonny Wilkinson. Myself and Ben Cohen were both screaming for the pass off Jonny but I must have been screaming the loudest because he passed to me - and the rest you know. I went over in the corner and you probably saw for yourself how all the emotion came out when I punched the ball into the air.

"I am told that the fans back home were a bag of nerves when the match went into extra time but I can promise you that the players weren't. We genuinely believed that we were playing a team of tired men. Our fitness was superior to Australia's and that's what got us through in the end.

"Admittedly we left it late but if there is one player in the world you would trust to land a drop-goal in the dying seconds of a World Cup final it would be Jonny Wilkinson. From the moment it left his foot we all knew it was going over."

The ecstatic celebrations on the pitch when the final whistle confirmed England as World Champions, the party into the early hours of the following morning, and that amazing welcome home at Heathrow which woke up sleeping birds for miles around. Will all that soon become no more than a pleasant, fading memory?

Will the status quo of this country's sporting life quickly be resumed with rugby union playing second fiddle once again to professional soccer and it's pop-star participants?

Robinson bristles at the very suggestion.

"I genuinely believe that what we achieved in Australia will raise the popularity of rugby union in this country to an entirely new level," he insists.

"And I don't just mean for the next few weeks until the World Cup memories have faded - I mean for good. The way rugby union is played and supported is completely different to soccer.

"Yes, rugby union is a very physical game played by some huge and powerful men. But do you ever see a player try to get another player into trouble in rugby union or any rugby union player bad-mouthing a referee? It just doesn't happen in my sport.

"And there is a completely different atmosphere among the crowd at a rugby union match. The two sets of supporters sit together.

"Yes, they enjoy a bit of light-hearted banter with each other but there is never any trouble among the rival fans.

"There were some massive crowds during the finals in Australia and there wasn't one arrest made inside a ground. That tells you everything.

"I have four kids of my own and if they are going to watch a match I want them to be going into a safe environment. I know they will be safe watching a rugby union match and I believe there are a lot of mums and dads throughout this country who are now thinking the same thing.

"I am convinced that we will see an upsurge in the number of kids coming into rugby union and in the numbers who turn up to watch our club matches."

But what of Robinson himself now that he's reached the pinnacle of his playing career? Could he be walking around with a second World Cup winner's medal around his neck?

"It's impossible to say," he answers. "I am 29 now and by the time the next World Cup finals come around I will be 33. But if I don't make the next one, I won't complain. I've played for my country at both rugby codes and in each of them I've played in a World Cup final against Australia.

"If it's the only one I win I will still thank God and count my blessings."

*

SUMMER OF SPORT

*Remember when we used to have summers? Here is a little something I
knocked up a few years ago which may illustrate how times have changed.
Somewhat prophetic this one. I even forecast that England were going to
wallop Australia in the Ashes, well too many Murphy's does that to you.*

FUN IN THE SUN

OF COURSE, IT might be my over-active imagination. Or the
Murphy's. Or a combination of both. But am I alone in thinking
that this is turning out to be the weirdest summer in years?

Even the weather has gone mad. By my reckoning, we've had
one genuinely hot day in June. You know the sort I'm talking about.
When you can fry an egg on the pavement. When you open the
door of your car and the blast of heat singes your eyebrows.

And how did that blistering day end? The rescue services were
airlifting people out of the tops of trees or off their roof because
there was a raging torrent sweeping away everything in its path.

Is that going to happen everytime the temperature gets into
the 80s this summer? I'm going to take precautions. I'm going to
nip out to the Army and Navy store and buy a dinghy for me and
the dog.

Neither of us can swim. The cat will have to fend for himself
but he's good at climbing trees.

Maybe it's on account of the heat but sport has gone a bit
doolally as well. How did the words of that old song go? "Give me
the crazy lazy hazy days of summer."

Well, we certainly got crazy right enough.

I'll let you into a little secret. In normal circumstances, I
wouldn't walk across the street to watch Formula One. A bunch
of maniacs charging around and around in ever-decreasing circles
before finally disappearing up their own exhausts.

But I tuned in to watch the United States Grand Prix in Indianapolis. It was what those who work in the arts refer to as the "theatre of embarrassment." Absolutely toe-curling and compulsive viewing for that reason.

There were more cars parked up in the garage than took part in the race. What a complete fiasco. No wonder the Yanks were lining up in their thousands demanding their money back.

It's too complicated to go into in detail here because when it was explained to me, my eyes glazed over. But basically, the majority of the drivers whose cars were fitted with a certain brand of tyre believed the track was too dangerous. Formula One officials turned down their request to switch to a different tyre and also rejected an alternative request to make the track safer.

One, or both, of those requests should have been accepted. They came from the drivers themselves. Men who put their life on the line each time they get behind the wheel for a race. I may have earlier referred to those drivers as maniacs, but not for one moment do I question their bravery. Those Formula One officials are idiots. Whoever coined the phrase "lions led by donkeys" had those officials in mind when he did so.

It's not all been petrol fumes and drivers who won't drive this summer. Wimbledon is with us. Shapely legs and lustrous blond locks. And some of the girls are a bit tasty as well!

Strawberries and cream at a price only the Loophole Lawyer and his clients can afford. You wouldn't catch me forking out an arm and a leg for a punnet. Strawberries give me wind. Nobody would sit within 10 feet of me.

Straight away there was another of those summer shocks I've been talking out. Nine Brits out of the Wimbledon Championships on day one. You could have knocked me down with a feather. ONLY nine? Blimey we must be getting better at the game. Normally by the second day only Tim Henman is left.

Of course, Tiger Tim is still in there grunting away as I write these words. Did you see his match against Jarkko Nieminen?

I've met Tim and he's a lovely lad. But when he gets on a tennis court, he's a ham. I reckon he does it on purpose just to keep us on the edge of our seats.

Two sets down against an opponent in 70th place in the world rankings. Do me a favour. If Tim wasn't playing to the crowd he would have beaten young master Jarkko in straight sets with one arm tied behind his back.

Look to your laurels, Timothy, there's a new British kid on the block by the name of Andy Murray who is about to steal your thunder. And after watching him in the pre-Wimbledon tournament at Queen's, it's clear that he's already a better actor than you are.

Cricket, lovely cricket. The addictive sound of leather on willow. If I don't get a written guarantee before I pop off that there's cricket in Heaven, then I'll take my chance of going to another place that's a damn sight hotter.

Football, by and large, is what I write about. Cricket is my sporting passion. I don't like cricket, oh no, I love it (10CC. No idea when).

But even cricket has gone barmy this summer. What odds would you have given me a couple of weeks ago on Bangladesh beating Australia? No disrespect to the Bangladeshi lads but that was the equivalent of Droylsden beating Arsenal in the FA Cup final.

But wasn't it absolutely wonderful to watch the cocky Aussies being humbled? Couldn't have happened to a nicer bunch of fellows.

I watched the Aussie captain Ricky Ponting as he walked off the square at Cardiff. He looked like he'd been bashed over the head with a mallet. Totally stunned and as miserable as sin. And his team-mates all had faces like a bulldog who had swallowed a wasp as well. The most delicious sight I've seen since I spied on the girl next-door sunbathing in the back garden in a skimpy bikini.

Of course, the "unbeatable" Aussies, the undisputed world champions and the greatest cricket team to grace this planet, got their comeuppance when they met our lads. But that was only to be expected. Because we've got so many world-class cricketers that we don't know what to do with them all.

We've got a kid with a skunk hair-do called Kevin Pietersen who smashed the Aussie attack out of sight last Sunday and didn't even get a bat when we hammered Bangladesh two days later.

And in both those English victories, Freddie batted like a drain. What's my number one sporting hero going to do to McGrath and company when he gets his eye in? I told you that this has been a crazy summer and it's going to get crazier.

If I was Ponting, I'd be afraid. I would be very afraid. Because Freddie, Harmy, the Skunk and the rest are coming to get you.

Australia are about to be dethroned. We will take back the Ashes this summer. Trust me on this one. I might be a bit wonky with my football predictions from time to time. But on all things cricket I'm infallible.

And you are getting the benefit of my encyclopaedic knowledge of the greatest game ever invented.

So when you see Michael Vaughan holding up the Ashes trophy later this summer, just remember where you read it first.

*

THE FINAL PINK

THE BIBLE FOR SPORTS FANS

In its glory days the Pink was selling 300,000 copies in one hour on a Saturday evening. By 2005 it wasn't even selling 30,000 so it had to go. How can you compete with TV, radio and all the new technology? The answer is you can't - here are my memories of the best sporting paper in the country.

FOR me, and I suspect for many, many more in and around this city who are no longer in the first flush of youth, it's like the death of a loved one after a long illness. You accept the inevitability but it doesn't ease the sadness.

And recording the passing into history of *The Football Pink* is one of the saddest duties I've had to perform in over three decades as a sports journalist on the *Manchester Evening News*. I truly feel as though I'm losing an old friend.

In its time and in its pomp, *The Saturday Pink* was without question the finest newspaper of its kind in this country. In the world of professional football throughout the sixties and seventies it was universally referred to as 'the Bible'. If you read it in the *Pink*, it had to be true.

Arguments on the field about whether that dubious goal should have counted were always settled the same way: "You don't think that was a goal? Read the *Pink* tonight, mate. Then you'll see if it was a goal or not."

Managers would come and managers would go. But wherever they went, they had to take 'the Bible' with them. *The Football Pink*'s mailing list 30 or 40 years ago read like a managerial Who's Who.

When Brian Green, the chatty, funny manager of Rochdale, left Spotland to take up the appointment of head coach with the Australian national team, *The Football Pink* went with him. Every

Monday morning, the previous Saturday's *Pink Final* was winging its way to Brian's home in Sydney - and he got it free of charge.

David Pleat, as manager at Luton Town in the seventies, told me he couldn't do his job without *The Football Pink* which he maintained had found more players for him than his entire scouting team.

"I've never got any money to spend," he told me at the time. "So I get *The Football Pink* sent to me every week and I pore through the non-league pages. I make a note of any player who gets a favourable mention - he could be at Stalybridge Celtic or Altrincham - and then dispatch one of my scouts to have a look at him in action. You would be surprised how many players I've signed out of the pages of the *Pink*."

My introduction to *The Football Pink* when I first joined this newspaper right at the start of the seventies was bizarre, to say the least. Because I actually wrote the report in the Saturday evening *Pink* of the match I was playing in.

I should explain that when I first set foot inside these offices on Deansgate, I was winding down my disastrous career as a professional footballer by playing on a part-time basis with Macclesfield Town, who were then in the old Northern Premier League. Because of my commitments at the Moss Rose, the *Evening News* very kindly gave me each Saturday off. A football writer who didn't have to work on Saturdays. Now that's what I call considerate employers.

Came one Saturday and a mini-crisis cropped up. Our Macclesfield correspondent who wrote the match reports for the Football Pink was suddenly taken ill and a replacement reporter could not be found in time. So, even though I was playing for Macc that afternoon, I was asked to step into the breach. All that was required, I was told, was three paragraphs at half-time and three more on the final whistle. Well, the Silkmen were a non-league club in those days, remember.

So in that Saturday night's Football Pink the Macclesfield Town versus Boston United match report was written by Macc's right-winger - dictated down the phone at half-time and full-time from the office of the club secretary.

Every one of those six paragraphs started with the name Hince. "Hince dazzled the crowd with another high-speed dash down the right. Hince left three defenders tackling fresh air with a mazy dribble."

We won 4-0 and I never mentioned any of the scorers because I wasn't one of them. Sheer reporter paradise.

I can still remember my first proper match report for *The Football Pink* more than 30 years ago. It was at Spotland - but I haven't the foggiest who Rochdale were playing that Saturday afternoon.

To my novice mind, this was football reporting as it should be. Instantaneous. A blow-by-blow account delivered down the phone while the match was in progress and typed out with mind-boggling speed by one of the copy-taking team in the *Evening News* offices.

And it was speed which made *The Football Pink* so unique. The whole operation in producing that newspaper was breathtaking. In fact, I'm still not sure how it was accomplished.

What I do know is that *Evening News* journalists like myself would finish our match reports at around a quarter-to-five on a Saturday evening. By five o'clock *The Football Pink* would be rolling off the presses complete with full match reports and every full-time score from every match in the country. Defies logic, doesn't it? But it happened every week.

By the time the Town Hall clock had stopped chiming out five o'clock, *The Football Pink* was already on sale at every street corner in Manchester's city centre. Less than an hour later it was available at your local newsagents in Macclesfield, Altrincham or Bury

Hard for the kids of today to picture it, but early Saturday evening when *The Football Pink* was due became a ritual for thousands and thousands of football supporters right around the region now known as Greater Manchester.

In the outlying districts, you would see queues snaking out of every newsagent's shop as supporters waited for that van loaded with copies of *The Football Pink* . No newsagent would close before the *Pink* arrived – not so much from a duty to their customers, but because it was nice little earner.

I can recall talking to my local newsagent some time in the seventies. He explained that when dad popped in at around six o'clock on a Saturday evening, he didn't only buy his *Football Pink*. Dad would buy his ounce of tobacco – maybe a nice box of chocolates for the missus and a bag of mixed sweets for the kids. Probably just to keep them all quiet while he read how United had played at Arsenal. But certainly profitable for the newsagent.

Of course that speed of production carried an element of danger. There was little or no time to correct any mistakes that cropped up from time to time in those scores of match reports that filled the pages of *The Football Pink*. So in one match report I sent from Gigg Lane my "ricochet" appeared that evening in the *Pink* as "Rick O'Shea"... John's great uncle, perhaps?

Another comical blunder with words was entirely of my own doing. This is what I said – and was printed in *The Football Pink* – in my report on an Oldham Athletic match at Boundary Park.

"Latics keeper Goram took a kick in the most sensitive part of his anatomy which led to a mad scramble in the penalty area for the loose ball." Now that really must have been painful!

Throughout the fifties, sixties and seventies, sales of *The Football Pink* were quite phenomenal – even more astonishing when you consider that the overwhelming majority of those sales were made in the space of one hour.

In those boom times for the *Pink*, our circulation department were fond of producing graphs which charted the sales figures for our Saturday evening sports paper. I looked at the figures for 1968 when City won the First Division title and United came back from

Wembley with the European Cup.

Sales of *The Football Pink* had, quite literally, soared off the page containing that graph. We couldn't print enough copies to meet the demand.

Our boffins in the circulation department also unearthed another curio. After conducting an extensive reader survey in the early seventies they discovered that a sizeable chunk of United fans did not buy *The Football Pink* when their team had lost, but City fans bought the paper on a Saturday evening win, lose or draw. You can make what you like of that.

To explain the success of *The Football Pink* during those boom years, bear in mind that three or four decades ago, a Saturday evening sports paper had virtually no competition.

Sure, football fans could pick up the results in those days from radio or television - but that was it. It was *The Football Pink* which provided the meat for those bones. Detailed match reports and analysis. And all that scarcely an hour after the match had ended. No wonder we saw those queues outside every newsagent's shop.

But the world has moved on since those golden days for Saturday evening sports papers. Now, by 5.30pm on a Saturday evening, every football fan knows everything he needs to know about how the team he supports has fared that afternoon.

Through television, or radio, computer or even mobile phone, by early Saturday evening in these high-tech times, that football fan knows his team's result, who scored, the views of the respective managers and, quite possibly, what the centre-forward is buying his girlfriend for her birthday present.

How can a Saturday evening sports paper compete with all that technology? The answer is glaringly obvious. It can't.

It is one of the prices we pay for progress but, to my mind, it's a heavy and unbearably sad price to pay.

Do you know what I'm thinking right now? I'm wishing it was 35 years ago and me and *The Football Pink* were starting out all over again. But that's me being sentimental and showing my age.

I know I can't turn back the hands of time and I've got to say goodbye to an old friend. But, believe me, that doesn't make the task any easier.

In all the years I've done this job, I've never finished writing an article with a heavier heart.

★

THE DEATH OF GEORGE BEST

FAREWELL

Me, George Best and Brian Kidd go back a long way. We played at the same time in the mid-sixties but I never held it against them for wearing red instead of blue.

George's death hit both of us hard and this was Kiddo's emotional tribute to his pal when George passed away in November 2005.

You will also read here of my tribute to an old friend and, arguably, the Greatest Footballer of All Time.

An emotional Brian Kidd last night said a tearful goodbye to his old friend and team-mate George Best, describing the Manchester United legend as "the greatest player I've ever seen in my life."

Collyhurst-born Kidd, who scored a goal on his 19th birthday while playing alongside Best in the Reds' historic European Cup final victory over Benfica in 1968, has been deeply affected by the death of the Irish genius yesterday. More so, perhaps, because he himself stared death in the face when he was diagnosed with prostate cancer from which he has made a full recovery.

"George was only three years older than me when I joined United in 1964 but he was already a huge star in the first team at Old Trafford," he recalled. "I can remember he played in the Youth Cup final that year when we beat Swindon Town and only a few days earlier he had been playing for Northern Ireland in a full international. That just wouldn't happen today, would it?

"With George in the team, United's youth side had beaten City a few weeks earlier in the semi-final of the Youth Cup. Years later there was a book written about that semi-final, *George Best and 21 Others*, which just about summed up George's contribution in that match. He was simply unstoppable.

"I used to watch him in training and he was quite unbelievable. In most of those training games you play one or two-touch football.

"George could beat his marker without having even one touch. He let his body do the work without touching the ball. I've never seen anything like it before or since.

"By the time I was halfway through my apprenticeship at Old Trafford, George was already a superstar. Probably the most famous footballer in the country.

"But you would never have guessed it from the way he behaved when he was around the other lads at the club. He was very shy and courteous to everyone, young or old. His mum and dad must have been so proud of him.

"There were no airs and graces about George. He would open a new boutique or whatever, in a blaze of publicity and then the next he would go into Old Trafford and hand out all manner of products to the apprentice players. I think everyone at the club, from top to bottom absolutely adored him.

"I was fortunate enough be in the same team as George when he was running riot on the pitch in the late 60s. I had a long career and played alongside, and against, some great players. Players who you could truly rate as world class.

"But none of them compared to George. He was certainly the greatest player of my lifetime.

"I'm a kid from Collyhurst so I didn't mix in the same circles George did. I certainly didn't rub shoulders with film stars and Miss Worlds. But George never forgot his roots or his old friends. In his mind he was always the kid from the back streets of Belfast.

"Obviously our paths went separate ways when he left Old Trafford. I was shocked and deeply saddened that he should leave the club when he was still only 26. But George was his own man. He wanted to live the life of his choosing and I have never criticised him for that.

"Of course all those tales about his drinking began to surface after he left Old Trafford but, with hand on heart, I can honestly say that in all the times I met George after he left United, never once had I seen him drunk.

"I still remember the time when we were both playing in America in the early 80s. By then there were stories in the papers every day that George's drinking was out of control.

"We were due to play George's team San Jose and he sent me a message, asking me to visit him. He had found an English bar run by an Englishman where they served fish and chips. And that's how we spent the evening, playing darts and eating fish and chips. George never touched a drop of alcohol all night.

"I don't want to make an issue about George's drinking. I do know that he was highly intelligent and if he did develop a habit he couldn't control, it wouldn't have reached that stage without him fighting with all his might against it.

"I hope and believe that people will remember him for what he was in his prime. Certainly the greatest player of his generation and possibly the greatest player of all time. That, I'm sure, is how Manchester United fans will remember him.

"I will remember him as one of the most famous faces on the planet whom I shared a plate of fish and chips with in an English bar in America and as a decent human being who was blessed with a God-given football talent."

*

MY TEARS FOR A HERO AND FRIEND

SO, Georgie Boy had one last surprise up his sleeve for the watching world – he actually turned up for his own funeral. Don't worry. That's not me disrespecting the memory of George Best. But knowing him as I did, I'll guarantee he would have loved to have been somewhere else last Saturday morning.

That would have appealed to his wicked sense of humour. All

those people lining the streets of the council estate where he was brought up in Belfast. The rich and the famous squeezed into the main hall at Stormont Castle. And the very man they had all come to honour and remember wasn't even there. George would have split his sides laughing at that.

You see, throughout his life-time GB had a habit of going "missing". He used to joke about it when he was making an after-dinner speech ... Miss World, Miss Great Britain, Miss USA. In the next breath he would deny that he'd had romantic liaisons with SEVEN Miss Worlds. "It was only three," he would insist. "I didn't turn up for the other four". Still, three Miss Worlds. Not bad, eh? Boy did George have a way with women.

George, as I remember, was invariably missing when I was ghost-writing his weekly column for this newspaper back in the seventies. We would arrange a time and a place for our weekly chat but he hardly ever turned up. It would have been easier ghost-writing Lord Lucan.

Oh, I'd find him in the end, of course, usually at about three in the morning in the Slack Alice nightclub just a goal-kick away from *Manchester Evening News* headquarters in the city centre.

I can recall him telling me at the time about one of his famous disappearing acts which nearly got him banned for life from setting foot inside any branch of a household name high street store.

The store in question was opening a new, state-of-the-art branch in Dublin. The deal was that George would be jetted over to the Republic's capital and booked into Dublin's finest hotel.

The following morning he would be driven to the city's main shopping street in the back of a white, open-topped Rolls Royce and he would officially open the new branch by cutting a ribbon draped across the main entrance with a pair of giant, golden scissors.

That was all George had to do. No speeches. No pressing the flesh. Just cutting the ribbon with those ceremonial scissors. And for that he would receive a fee of £5,000 which, I'm guessing, was around a full year's pay for an average working man back in those days.

George was flown out to Dublin, as arranged. He did spend the night in that luxurious hotel. He did clamber into the back of that white, open-topped Rolls Royce the following morning. The car did drive him onto Dublin's main shopping street - at which point George tapped the driver on the shoulder and ordered him to turn the car around and take him back to the airport to board the next flight to Manchester.

My jaw dropped open while George was telling me that story.

"So you never cut the ribbon? "I asked.

"No, I never did," he replied.

"And you never got your £5,000?" I continued.

"No, I never did," came back the reply

"After going to all that trouble, why didn't you go through with it?" was the next obvious question.

George shrugged his shoulders as though he had just lost 50p. "I saw all those people waiting for me outside that store and I just couldn't be bothered," he said. "I had a bit of a hangover that morning."

That was the George Best I got to know and like back in the seventies. Easy come, easy go. He never had more than a fleeting acquaintance with money. Here today, gone tomorrow. Looking back on it, you could say pretty much the same about his girlfriends back in the days when his face was one of the most recognisable on planet earth.

It's funny how little half-forgotten tales like his non-opening of that store in Dublin came flooding back while I was watching pictures of his funeral service on Saturday morning.

Mind you, even the wording is not quite right, is it? More of a state funeral than a personal funeral. If the rest of the world wanted to know what the people of Belfast really thought about THEIR

George, then Saturday morning gave them the answer. He was their hero. Their hope and inspiration during The Troubles that brought that city to its knees. They adored him and they will never, ever forget him.

Having known and liked George enormously for more than forty years, I wasn't sure how I would react when I watched him being finally laid to rest on Saturday morning. I thought I would be fine. After all his funeral was a celebration of the career of the greatest footballer I have had the privilege of watching in my lifetime. I had convinced myself before the service began at Parliament House that I would be able to rejoice in those wonderful memories of watching George at the very peak of his career.

I should have known better. My eyes were prickling before Denis Law had finished his tribute to his old friend and teammate. What was a trickle became a flood when George's son Calum broke down while reading a poem about his dad written by a neighbour and pushed through the letterbox of the Best's family home.

I couldn't watch any longer. The dog was taken for an unexpected walk. Let's hope the neighbours didn't spot me walking past with tears rolling down my face.

Those stronger than me may have regarded George's funeral as a celebration of a glorious career.

I just found it unbearably sad that a true footballing genius and a wonderfully warm human being had left us without even reaching his 60th birthday.

How should we remember George Best in the years to come? Perhaps there is no way to answer that question. Each generation will have different memories of George and - sadly - not all of them good.

I can only speak for myself because I'm of the same generation as the man who was laid to rest alongside his mother Ann in a Belfast graveyard.

I won't remember him for his excesses. In the years to come I won't remember George as a man who fought - and lost - his battle against alcoholism. I won't remember George who upset and offended the very people he loved most. That wasn't the real George doing those terrible things - that was the bottle.

I will remember him in his prime at Manchester United in the late sixties. Without question the finest footballer ever produced by the United Kingdom and, arguably the finest footballer of all time. The film-star looks that made me want to spit. The warmth and charm of his personality. The smile that could melt an ice-cube and the hearts of more pretty young girls than you could shake a stick at.

From the very first moment he caressed a football in front of an adoring public at Old Trafford when he was still a teenager, there was an indefinable magic about the Belfast Boy. Even his very name was a gift for the headline writers.

For reasons which no amount of words can explain, right from the very start of his career, George fascinated all manner of people in all walks of life. And, mysteriously that fascination never abated throughout his entire life.

Truly great players down the years have stepped back into obscurity once their playing days were over. Believe me, the current obsession with David Beckham will fade away when he's no longer kicking a football for a living.

With George, that never happened. Thirty years after turning his back on football, he was as famous and idolised in death as he ever was in life. There is no way to explain that phenomenon other than to say that there will only ever be one Georgie Best. Professional football will never see his like again. Rest in peace, George. And don't go turning up at United's next home match.

Well, it wouldn't do to break the habits of a lifetime, would it?

RICKY'S WORLD

He's as daft as a brush, an ardent Man City fan and addicted to "Only Fools and Horses". He's even got Del Boy's Yellow Robin Reliant in his back garden.

Of course it's Ricky Hatton I'm talking about and when I discovered he lives only five minutes away from the Garden City of Hazel Grove I popped along to meet him. Here is what I made of my meeting with 'the Hitman'.

If you didn't have specific instructions, you would drive right past it. Just a little street off a steep and narrow lane winding its way upwards towards Werneth Low Golf Club.

Hard to image that in a house on the bend in that little street there's someone waiting for you who, in the very near future, is going to be one of the most famous sportsmen on this planet.

As you pull up at the front door of that white painted house you are given your first clue about the identity of the occupier.

Outside is parked a black BMW with a number plate that reads "RIC Y-H." There is also an unmissable clue on a plaque on the wall by the side of the front door which tells you a lot about the occupier's taste in music. Written on that plaque are the words "Heart Break Hotel."

The young man I've come to meet welcomes me with a grin which wouldn't disgrace a Cheshire cat and ushers me into his magnificent ground-floor games room.

In here the clues to his identity almost assault the senses in the sheer volume and diversity of the souvenirs and mementos hanging from every wall.

Pictures everywhere of great Manchester City players past and present. Framed blue football shirts signed by Robbie Fowler and Ali Benarbia. Even the beize on the full-sized snooker table is light blue. If I tell you that there are also signed photographs on one wall of George Best and Alex Ferguson it will probably put you off the scent, so I won't mention them.

For every football souvenir on those walls there are two representing boxing. England caps and certificates acknowledging the eight national titles our mystery man won during his amateur career. Framed action shots featuring legendary fighters like Muhammad Ali and Mike Tyson.

But not all the souvenirs which cover virtually every inch of those walls are a celebration of sport. There's a signed photo of the "adult" comedian Roy Chubby Brown. And the occupier of this house is a "Fools and Horses" nut.

Another plaque welcomes you to "Nelson Mandela House, London Borough of Peckham." On another wall is a beautifully-drawn pencil sketch of Del Boy, Rodney and Grandad. The alarm clocks in the house wake you up to the "Fools and Horses" theme tune.

The occupier takes me through to the back garden and shows me one of his proudest possessions. It's one of the yellow Robin Reliants driven by the Trotters as they back-fired their way around the streets of London. And this one is in full working condition complete with its M.O.T.

All the clues are there. Elvis. Roy Chubby Brown. Only Fools and Horses. All things Manchester City And, oh yes, I nearly forgot. Wall-to-wall boxing. Have you guessed his identity yet?

Because if you haven't you will NEVER get that invitation to appear on "Through the Keyhole".

Of course you've guessed it. The young man waiting to welcome me at the front door of that house in the little street off that narrow lane was Manchester's very own world light-welterweight champion Ricky "The Hitman" Hatton.

Just under a fortnight ago at The MEN Arena in the wee small hours of a Sunday morning, the world changed for Ricky Hatton. It would be just as accurate to state that, in the same space of time,

Ricky Hatton changed the world.

That change came off the back of Hatton's ruthless demolition of one of the great boxing champions of modern times — the brave and dignified Australian Kostya Tszyu. And that victory will bring the global fame and the fortune that goes with it for one of Manchester's favourite sons.

Suddenly Hatton is big box office. Not just in Manchester but in Manhattan. Not just in Sunderland but in Sydney. Television companies are fighting for the rights to screen his future fights.

American boxing fans want to see the pocket-sized tornado in person. And to grant them that privilege, Hatton could name his own price to step into a ring on the other side of the Atlantic.

Barring a disaster of biblical proportions, Hatton's fists will earn him enough money over the next couple of years to ensure his financial security for the rest of his days. We all know by now what he's like inside the ring - an unstoppable explosion of controlled aggression.

But what is Manchester's newest world champion like OUTSIDE the ring? That is what I intended to find out when I pitched up at his front door yesterday.

First of all let me tell you that he is everything I hoped he would be - and more. You will never meet a world champion in any sport more down-to-earth, open, friendly or more downright likeable than Ricky Hatton. If it wasn't for his dad Ray, a former team-mate of mine at Manchester City, I would have kidnapped Ricky and adopted him.

Ricky was Ray and Carol's first child when he was born in Hattersley 27 years ago come next October. Some two years later the Hattons were blessed with another son, Matthew, who is already a Central Area champion. Matthew is the black sheep of the family — he supports that "other" club from Stretford.

"Because my dad was on the books at Maine Road before an injury ended his career it was natural that I should grow up as a

City fan," said Ricky.

"I was a fairly useful midfielder when I was a kid and represented Tameside schoolboys. And then I spent two years at City's School of Excellence and for a while I thought I might be following in my dad's footprints.

"But all the time I was being pulled towards boxing. That started when I took up kick-boxing when I was about 11. I was no good at that because my legs were too short but the sport did show me that I could punch.

"I started boxing as an amateur at a local club in Hattersley and later joined the Sale West Club. I picked up the Hitman nickname right at the start of my amateur career. I was doing some work on the punch-bag and I was really going at it hammer and tongues, which is what I'm like once I get my gloves on. One of the trainers said "Blimey, we've got a right little hitman here" and the tag has stuck to me ever since.

"By the time I was 15 I had already won four national titles but suddenly the fights started to dry up. I was knocking kids of my own age out inside a minute and no-one wanted to fight me.

"I spent so much time chasing fights that I hardly attended City's School of Excellence and in the end the club decided to let me go.

"But as things turned out, that was the best thing that ever happened to me."

Away from the ring and when he's not wandering around Hyde in his yellow Robin Reliant, Hatton spends as much time as he can with his four-year-old son Campbell, who he quite clearly adores.

Sadly his relationship with his son's mother Claire failed to be a lasting one.

"I went to Mottram Primary School to begin my education and Campbell is starting at the same school in September," said a proud Hatton.

"He doesn't live with me but I see him every day and we are very close. Even when I'm in training, I make sure that I get a couple of hours off so that we can be together.

"I've been a professional since I turned 18 and for the last few years I've been chasing fights against the top welterweights," he added.

"Now I am the world champion and it is their turn to chase me. I can pick and choose my opponents and I only want to match myself against the best.

"I will go to fight in America but only because that's my choice. I think every boxer dreams of topping the bill at a venue in Las Vegas.

"But I would never turn my back on my fans in Manchester because they have helped put me where I am today. For the fight against Tszu at the M.E.N. Arena all 22,000 tickets were sold in three hours. There isn't another boxer anywhere in the world who can count on support like that.

"Of course finances dictate that you've got to take the America market into consideration. The fights I have in Manchester have to be staged in the early hours of the morning so that they can be shown live on prime-time TV in America. That's what makes the big money.

"I don't want to over-stay my welcome in boxing. I intend to go on for another two or three years with maybe six or seven more fights and then call it a day

"And once I've retired I intend to stay retired. I don't think there is anything sadder than seeing a once great fighter coming out of retirement through boredom or lack of money and then getting a good hiding because he's past his best.

"That isn't going to happen to me. I've got good advisers and a strong family around me. My dad looks after my finances and he will make sure that the future will be secure when the time comes for me to hang up my gloves.

"I do have a couple of ambitions to aim for apart from the obvious one of retiring as reigning world champion. I would love to fight at least once at the City of Manchester Stadium. That would be another dream come true for me and for my family.

"And I want to watch City playing in Europe within the next two or three years. Why not? If Everton can do it, then so can we.

"And I think we can do it under Stuart Pearce. Just think of it. Me retiring as the unbeaten world champion and City winning the Champions League. Well, at least one out of two is possible."

★

WAYNE ROONEY

FORTY years ago, during the summer of 1966, I drove over to Goodison Park with my pal and Manchester City team-mate Tony Coleman to watch Brazil playing in the group stage of the World Cup finals.

There were two reasons why me and TC travelled over to watch that match. The first was that we got in for nowt. In those days, players just had to produce their club pass confirming their identity to gain free admission at every ground in the country. Nice little wheeze, that.

The second, more pertinent reason, was that both of us were desperate to see Pele in the flesh. We had heard and read so much about the greatest player on the planet and the opportunity to watch him in action live for the very first time was simply irresistible.

But had we not known that the great man always wore the No 10 shirt, we would not have been aware that Pele was in the Brazilian team that night. He was smothered right out of the game. As wise-cracking Tony said, "you wouldn't have been able to spot him with the help of radar".

We were both disappointed that we hadn't watched Pele at

his brilliant best. But we weren't unduly surprised. We both played football for a living - one well and the other badly - so we understood. Even the greatest footballer in the world is entitled to the occasional off-day. I think it has something to do with being human.

That brings me to Wayne Rooney, who I suppose could be described as the Pele of English football. I've watched him in his last two appearances for Manchester United, against Celtic and Arsenal, and I'll guarantee that in both those matches he would have been disappointed with his own performance.

His frustration was particularly evident in Sunday's defeat against the Gunners. He wasn't disinterested, because that's not in his character. But he looked dispirited. Nothing was happening for him. It's an odd thing about football. Sometimes the harder you try, the worse you play.

And, of course, on the strength of those two displays, the barm-pots have come out of the woodwork. Yesterday, I trawled through the fans' forum on Ceefax. It was all there as I expected.

Rooney is not all he's cracked up to be. He's a busted flush. When did he last score in a competitive match for England? He's too big for his boots. Page after page of drivel.

If Rooney bothered to read those comments, I hope he burst out laughing, because they are not worth taking seriously.

Harder to ignore, though, are the comments made about Rooney at the weekend by his former Old Trafford team-mate Roy Keane, who said that the young Liverpudlian had achieved nothing of any great significance in his career so far.

Roy Keane has said that Wayne Rooney had "achieved nothing" and that he had still got "a hell of a lot to do" and "potential is one thing, doing it another." And in reply to this Paul Hince writing in the *Manchester Evening News* today says "even Pele had his off days".

The comparision to Pele may remind some of big Phil

Scolari's very original response when he was asked if he saw any comparison between Rooney and Pele. "One is white, the other is black. Rooney is an excellent player but Pele is unique. There will never be another Pele – not for a thousand years and not even in a computer game."

Publicly questioning Mad Dog's judgement can be bad for your health, so if you don't hear from me for the next few weeks, then you'll know why – because I'm going to disagree with Roy Keane.

Within weeks of completing his education, the boy Rooney was competing against men in the Premiership for Everton. At such a tender age, he didn't just hold down a place in the senior side at Goodison Park. He was far and away Everton's best player. That was a huge achievement.

In 2004, while he was still only 18, United boss Ferguson splashed out the best part of £30m to bring Rooney to the Theatre of Dreams. It was a measure of the youngster's obvious talent that Fergie was prepared to pay such a vast amount for a player of that age. To be able to attract such a massive offer from arguably the biggest club in the world was a huge achievement.

At 17, Rooney was called into England's senior squad. He took to the highest level of professional football so well, he is now regarded as indispensable to England's national team. That was a huge achievement.

Ferguson has a galaxy of stars at Old Trafford. None has shone more brightly this past couple of years than Rooney. As he is for England, so he has become for United. Indispensable.

So that's where Keane and I part company. He thinks Rooney has achieved little in his career so far; I think the boy has achieved masses. And he's only just begun. So I hope he's not too harsh on himself, because of a couple of indifferent performances. Always bear in mind, Wayne, that while form ebbs and flows, quality endures. And you've got 24-carat quality oozing out of every pore.

FC UNITED

NOW here is a story that has put a smile back on the face of a cynical old scribbler. FC United moving up in the world after gaining promotion in their very first season in business. Congratulations to manager Karl Marginson and his bonny team.

But more than anything, I would like today to doff my cap to the fans of the club formed as a direct result of the Glazer takeover at Old Trafford. Take a bow every last one of you. As true football supporters go, the fans of FC United are Premiership class.

I still remember driving through a monsoon last August to watch FC's first competitive match against Leek SCOB who normally attract an attendance of 70 paying customers, two dogs and a ginger tom.

But more than 3,000 spectators were crammed into Leek's modest headquarters. My guess is that 2,900 of them were FC United fans. And they were magnificent.

As I drove back towards Macclesfield along the Leek Road that day I recall thinking that it would never last. It gives me enormous pleasure to admit that I was wrong. When promotion was clinched with a 4-0 victory over Chadderton on Wednesday, FC were roared on by 2,788 fans inside Gigg Lane. That is 40 times greater than any other club at that level can attract.

What lies in waiting for FC United over the years to come I have no way of knowing. What I do know is that this won't be their last promotion. This is a club going places. How could it be any different? With wonderful fans like that behind them, the sky's the limit.

FROM THE LA TIMES - 19TH MAY 2005

Paul Hince, Chief Sportswriter for the *Manchester Evening News*, said the purchase of the club was understandable because 'as a money-making concern, the Old Trafford empire is just about as good as it gets". Nevertheless, he said, he had grave misgivings about Glazer.

"A resident of Tampa Bay, Fla., he has no background in football and no feel for the traditions and history of the club he now owns. Has he heard of Duncan Edwards? Does he know what Munich means, other than it's a city in Germany? I very much doubt it".

*

SIR TAGGART

In 2004 the reds failed to win the Premiership (for once) and all the loonies came out from under their stones to take a pot-shot at the manager.

Here is my response to the nit-wits coupled with a tribute to the Chelsea manager Claudio (the tinkerman) Ranieri for his wonderful sense of humour as he faced the axe from Roman (the Butcher) Abramovich.

DON'T WRITE HIM OFF

IF results go their way Manchester United could end this season as runners-up in the Premiership and holders of the FA Cup. Now, if those were the targets within the reach of a certain other club in Manchester, supporters of a Blue persuasion would be floating around on Cloud Nine right now demanding a knighthood for King Kevin.

But a Champions' League spot next season and the FA Cup on the sideboard at Old Trafford isn't good enough for the Red hordes, is it?

Whatever happens over the next couple of weeks, in their eyes this season has been one long let-down. And the United supporters are never backward at coming forward, are they, when they've got something to gripe about?

We've all heard it. Fergie has lost the plot. He's too old. Never should have sold Beckham. He's lost the dressing-room. His signings wouldn't get into Hartlepool's first-team.

Gorblimey O'Riley!

Those fans will be blaming Sir Taggart for the weather next.

It's absolute cobblers, of course. The Fiery One hasn't lost the plot. He's not too old. He was right to flog Beckham and he's not lost the dressing room.

Not so sure about the weather bit, though.

What is true, however, is that United's standards have slipped this season and I'm willing to bet that Fergie himself would be the first to confirm the accuracy of that statement.

But to my mind, that's not Ferguson's fault. It's not Rio Ferdinand's fault. It's not Roy Keane's fault and it's not Ryan Giggs's fault. In fact, it's not anyone's fault.

For what we've been witnessing at the Theatre of Dreams this season has not been the end of an era or the collapse of the Old Trafford Empire.

We've been watching the turn of a wheel as part of a natural cycle which occurs not only in professional football but in any other sport you care to name.

People of a certain age, like myself, will remember when the West Indian cricket team, with their battery of giant, super-quick bowlers, were literally invincible. But their cycle turned.

In cricket, as in soccer and as in life, nothing lasts forever.

Now it's the turn of Australia to rule the cricket world.

Let's move the clock forward to more modern times.

Not so long ago, Wigan were the Manchester United of Rugby League. They dominated their sport every bit as comprehensively as the Reds dominated English soccer. But the cycle rotated as it always does.

Now, it's Bradford Bulls who are the kings of Rugby League.

If you look back far enough into the history of professional soccer in this country you will find a period when Huddersfield Town were the most successful club in England. As you have perhaps realised, it didn't last.

Keep turning the pages and you'll see the theme repeating itself over and over again.

For a brief period in the late sixties, Manchester City's star shone brighter than any other at the top of English soccer. Nottingham Forest won the European Cup - twice - under Brian Clough's management.

For City and Forest - and a host of other clubs down the years

- their day in the sun came and went as part of the natural sequence of things.

Manchester United have been luckier than most.

Their cycle has been so slow to turn that we've hardly noticed it, and that has been due to Ferguson's extraordinary ability to dismantle one great side seamlessly and to build another without any jagged edges being visible to the naked eye.

But that couldn't last forever. It doesn't take much to move the cycle forward, you know. The years start to catch up with a couple of key players.

Others stars, after winning so much so often for so long, discover that they are no longer quite so hungry as they once were. Newcomers from abroad take longer than anticipated to adapt to the hurly-burly of the Premiership.

And before you know it, another club has nipped in to knock you off your pedestal.

So now the cycle has turned in Arsenal's favour.

It's their chance to take centre stage - their day in the sun. How long that day will last is impossible to predict.

But it won't last forever because history tells us so.

Sooner or later another club will reach and then exceed those high standards that Arsene Wenger's team have laid down in the Premiership this season.

Will that club be Manchester United?

I, for one, wouldn't bet against it. I'll wager a fiver against a pinch of the other that the old fire-breather who's currently smashing up the furniture in his cave over at Old Trafford will build one more championship-winning team before he stalks off into the sunset to tend his roses in the gardens at Dun Roamin in leafy Wilmslow.

★

CLAUDIO'S MY NO 1

FOR as long as I can remember I've never given a monkey's about the fortunes of Chelsea Football Club.

Well, it's a London club isn't it? And when it comes to London clubs, I'm completely impartial. I don't care who beats 'em.

But this season I've grown quite fond of Chelsea and I suspect you might be feeling the same.

If you do, it will only be for one reason, won't it? Their manager Claudio Ranieri. What a brilliant geezer.

I can't think of any other manager, foreign or otherwise, who has earned the affection of the entire nation in the way Ranieri has since arriving at Stamford Bridge.

What's happened to old Claudio since Russian owner Roman Abramovich and Peter Kenyon joined forces you wouldn't wish on your worst enemy.

But Ranieri has taken it all on the chin with unfailing dignity and a wonderfully black sense of humour.

I split my sides laughing when Ranieri was interviewed after Chelsea's Champions League match in Monaco where his club's owner had his sumptuous sea-going yacht berthed in the harbour.

"Mr Abramovich invited me onto his yacht after the match," said straight-faced Claudio, "he wanted to use me as the anchor."

How can you not love a man and a manager with a sense of humour like that? And as far as I'm concerned, Abramovich and Kenyon deserve locking up in the Tower of London for the shameful way they've treated Ranieri these past few months.

Actually a part of me is quite pleased that Roman and his Enforcer are going to show Ranieri the exit door in a couple of week's time and replace him with the Porto boss Jose Mourinho whose ego is the size of Big Ben.

Because with Claudio out of the way I can go back to hating Chelsea with a vengeance.

★

Alex Ferguson's eyes lit up when he spotted me at a United Press Conference ahead of a Champions League match in Bucharest.

Every time I asked him a question he burst out laughing. That's no way to treat a liverish old hack so this became a column which provided plenty of questions from yours truly but no answers from the Fiery One.

10 ROUNDS WITH SIR TAGGART

RIGHT from the moment the plane touched down at Bucharest's international airport yesterday I knew I was going to have trouble with Alex Ferguson. Sir Taggart hadn't noticed me on the flight out from Manchester. The big cheeses from Old Trafford were sat at the front travelling business class. The hacks were herded together in the cheap seats at the back.

Mind you, I was happy about that. Well have you ever heard of a plane backing into a mountain? But the Fiery One noticed me alright when we landed in Bucharest. His eyes almost popped out of their sockets. "You," he spluttered. "You. What are You doing here? Can't get into Europe vith your own team so you have to latch onto us. Well I'm telling you nowt you Little Blue spy!" Nice to be made welcome, isn't it? Within half-an-hour I was face-to-face again with the old fire breather. This time it was at the official press conference in United's Bucharest hotel. The Hilton is where the Reds are staying ahead of tonight's Champions League qualifier. And very nice it is, too. I wish I had booked in there myself. Now that really would have cooked Fergie's goose wouldn't it?

But Sir Alex thinks it's all a laughing matter

Sir Taggart answered the first few questions with his usual mixture of courtesy and clarity so I thought I'd chip in with my own two pennies worth.

Well, the *Evening News* hadn't paid for me to come to Romania to sit here like a stuffed dummy.

You see, on the way out I'd heard that the pitch in the National Stadium where tonight's match will be staged leaves a bit to be desired.

In fact, if what I'd heard was true, there are better pitches in Debdale Park in January than the one which the Reds will be performing on tonight.

So I asked Fergie what I thought was an eminently sensible question.

"Manager," I said, "Is the condition of the pitch on which you will play the match against Dinamo a worry for you?"

Do you know what Taggart did? He burst out laughing. And everyone else in the press conference fell about laughing as well. I've not been so embarrassed since I chatted up a girl in a bar in Amsterdam and found out she was a fella.

"Oh it's a bad pitch alright," chortled Fergie, who was red in face by now after his laughing fit.

"It's as bad as the one your team plays on at the City of Manchester Stadium," (more gales of laughter from all and sundry).

The giggling knight of the realm didn't understand who he was dealing with. I've been mocked by experts. He wasn't going to silence the voice of the *Manchester Evening News*, so I tried again.

"Mister Manager," I said in a voice even firmer than before, "have you settled in your mind on the team you will field against Dinamo Bucharest?"

Do you know what Taggart did? He burst out laughing again. And everyone else in the press conference fell about laughing again. It was getting more and more like a Morecambe and Wise routine.

Finally Fergie pulled himself together sufficiently enough to give me an answer.

"You think you are talking to Kevin don't you?" he wheezed. "And Kevin would give you an answer wouldn't he? But you're not talking to Kevin and you ain't getting my team."

By now I had my dander up. Knight or not, the manager sat up there on the stage with the red face and the heaving shoulders wasn't going to get the better of me.

"Mister Ferguson," I demanded in my sternest voice, "are you going to burst out laughing every time I ask you a question while we are together in Bucharest?"

Do you know what Taggart did? Of course you know what he did. He burst out laughing. "That's it," he said, wiping the tears from he eyes, "press conference over."

Trust me on this one - I'm a journalist. He's not heard the last of this yet - and neither have you.

Before we leave Romanian soil I'm going to get a straight answer one way or the other out of Mr High and Mighty Alex Ferguson.

King Kevin would never dream of treating me this way!

★

Alex Ferguson doesn't make many mistakes but he dropped an almighty clanger in January 2006 when he picked the wrong team against the mighty blues - and paid the price for it.

The following day I took my life in my hands and criticised Fergie in print - and amazingly lived to tell the tale. Here is what I wrote.

YOU'RE TO BLAME, SIR ALEX

TRANSLATED into English, the Latin inscription on Manchester City's coat-of-arms says: Pride in Battle. And never have those words been more appropriate than in Saturday's Eastlands derby

For that's what these encounters between the old rivals are all about. Pride in the shirt you are wearing and a willingness to battle until you drop for the club and supporters you serve.

And that, in a nut-shell, is why Stuart Pearce's wonderful warriors so richly deserved to win the 134th league derby.

To a man the Blues oozed pride. Each and every one was up for the battle. Manchester United displayed neither of those qualities. And they also got what they so richly deserved - a good hiding.

Alex Ferguson picked the wrong target for his rant. Referee Steve Bennett didn't cost his side three points. It was his own players who did that for the most gutless display from a United side I can recall in a fixture that means so much.

Never mind blaming the referee for an opening City goal that may or may not have been offside. Never mind blaming him for red-carding Cristiano Ronaldo for a studs-first lunge at Andy Cole. Instead, Fergie should blame his players for amateurish defending you wouldn't expect to see in the Conference, and for their arrogance in believing that they could stroll their way to victory without breaking sweat.

And, if he's big enough and honest enough to admit that even the best of managers make mistakes, the Old Trafford boss might even blame himself for the defeat. For it can't be argued, surely, that Fergie's baffling team-selection played no small part in his team's derby downfall.

Introducing new signing Patrice Evra to English football in a Manchester derby was a justifiable gamble. The lad has got Champions League experience. Playing against a team which had picked up one measly Premiership point out of the last 12 shouldn't have held any terrors for him. On the day, Evra froze. He looked like a rabbit caught in a car's headlights. But Fergie wasn't to know how he would respond.

The more pertinent question to ask is why Ferguson chose to play Mikael Silvestre alongside Rio Ferdinand in preference to Wes Brown who, unquestionably, is the best natural defender and the best tackler on the pay-roll at Old Trafford.

The word going around the stadium was that Silvestre had been chosen to "talk" his fellow countryman Evra through his debut match. The logic in that escapes me. The language of football is universal. Good players don't need to be told where to go, who to mark and when to tackle. They do that by instinct.

And if Silvestre was selected solely to act as Evra's on-field interpreter, why was he not replaced at half-time when Ferguson decided that his new left-back would take no further part in proceedings? It was a selection that was baffling and disastrous in equal measure.

What's gone wrong with Silvestre I can't even begin to imagine. He just doesn't look the player he was of 12 months ago. Woefully short on confidence. Hesitant in the tackle. Nervous and uncertain in his passing. Fergie's big mistake wasn't in selecting his new Frenchman - it was in selecting his old Frenchman because Silvestre's jitters were contagious. In this particular derby United's entire back-four couldn't have defended their honour.

But perhaps it's wrong to dwell on United's shortcomings - and there were plenty of those. To do that would be to detract from a truly heart-warming display from Pearce's team which produced the tingling atmosphere inside the City of Manchester Stadium which Ferguson claimed didn't exist.

Pearce, proud as Punch after the match and every right to be so, refused to single out any of his players for special praise. And I can well understand why. It's not being disrespectful to the Blues to point out that United, as a team, have more quality within their ranks. Pearce admitted that much himself in his after-match Press briefing.

But when you've got 11 players working selflessly for each other, players winning tackles that they shouldn't win, players willing to run themselves into the ground for the cause, then you've got a team that can move mountains.

That was Manchester City. A team in every sense of the word. That was why Pearce wouldn't single out individuals. And against their arch-rivals from across town, Pearce's players proved what their manager knew all along. A team will beat 11 individuals every day of the week. Happily, there are no such restrictions on an ageing scribbler. I can single out individuals from an overall team performance by the Blues which was just about as good as it gets. My problem is where to start.

Let's start at the back and work our way up-field. If Fergie paid £5m for Evra, then how much is Stephen Jordan worth? Not a penny less in my book. For all his show-pony tricks, Ronaldo is still a handful if you give him time and space. On Saturday young Jordan gave him neither. Mind you, he gave the Spanish dance-master one or two bumps and bruises to count but, hey, this was a Manchester derby one of the few occasions when tackling is permitted.

Despite scoring a goal which, take note Fergie, also had a suspicion of off-side about it, Ruud van Nistelrooy was conspicuous mainly by his absence while young Master Rooney grew so frustrated that you could spot the steam coming out of his ample ear-holes from the back of the main stand.

The reason for van Nistelrooy's disappearing act and Rooney's growing temper? Both of them spent 90 minutes in the pocket of Sylvain Distin and 70 minutes in the pocket of Richard Dunne until the gallant Irish giant limped off with a damaged knee.

In midfield, Joey Barton's radar seemed to be on the blink when it came to picking out team-mates with his passing but that's a minor quibble. He more than made up for that with his work-rate. By the time referee Bennett blew the final whistle, Joey must have been on first-name terms with every blade of grass.

And don't be fooled by Stephen Ireland's appearance. He looks like a gust of wind would knock him over but you ask some of the beefier United players he clattered into without fear of his own safety. This young man is as tough as old boots. And other players would kill for his passing ability - what a player Ireland is going to be with a few more miles on his clock.

Up-front for the Blues, Andy Cole and Darius Vassell were

superb. What a pity Old King Cole couldn't get on the score-sheet against his old club. A goal might even have put a smile on his face.

And I certainly know what Vassell drinks before a match - rocket fuel. If they had opened the gates at Eastlands during Saturday's match Vassell would have been spotted five minutes later running down Deansgate.

And in keeping with the tradition of saving the best until the last, take a bow Trevor Sinclair. For a variety of reasons it's been a long time coming but against the Reds this was Sinclair back to his England best. Strong, positive, dangerous and creative. You name it, Sinclair had it in this derby - even with the world's biggest elastoplast wrapped around his bonce. A dark-horse for the World Cup finals? Don't rule him out if he carries on playing like this.

What a pity that City chairman John Wardle was confined to bed with a chest infection. What a treat you missed, John, but what a tonic it must have been even watching your team's performance on the goggle box. Get well soon, Mr Chairman -and stay well. And maybe stay away from Eastlands a bit more often on match days if that's what it takes to induce the sort of team performance we witnessed from Pearce's team which made every last City supporter proud to be Blue.

★

THE LEGACY OF MUNICH

I'm a lifelong Manchester City fan but I've never been a United hater. The headlines of the dreadful Munich Disaster in 1958 are still vividly imprinted on my mind and here is a column advising the Glazer family to respect the memories of the wonderful Busby Babes who tragically perished in the inferno at Munich airport.

Also there is a personal tribute to one of English soccer's Greatest Teams and players who perished before their time in that awful tragedy.

MUNICH PAIN STILL SO STRONG

THE GLAZER FAMILY, or at least the sons of patriarch Malcolm, insist they are well aware of the traditions and the history of Manchester United. I have no reason to doubt them - you don't spend that amount of money on anything without doing your homework on the purchase.

So it's safe to assume that the Glazer sons have either been told or have read about the blackest day in the history of the club they now own - the disaster at Munich Airport in February, 1958 which decimated the wonderful Busby Babes team.

However, what United's American owners are unlikely to have been told, or read, is what effect that infamous day had on this city as a whole and, in particular, on the wives and families of the Babes who died in that crash and on those who survived.

I could be of some small assistance to the Glazers about how the city of Manchester reacted to the Munich disaster. I was 13 at the time, a City fan then, as now. But as the news of that awful crash and the lives lost in it began to filter through, the colour of your scarf meant nothing. In an instant, Manchester became a united city - United in grief.

Somehow it's shocking for a 13-year-old boy to see grown men weeping in the street. But that's what I witnessed on that day back in 1958. Those were hard times and they were hard men. Many would have risked their lives without flinching when fighting for their country in World War Two.

And yet that's what I saw that day - grown men, some war veterans, some United fans, some City fans, some who perhaps had no interest in football at all. But they stood there on the streets in shocked silence reading about the dreadful event at Munich Airport on the front page of the *Manchester Evening News,* or the now defunct *Evening Chronicle,* with tears rolling down their cheeks. It was an image which burned its way into my memory for life.

So, even though I was an impressionable schoolboy at the time, I could - if asked - give the Glazer brothers a flavour of the overwhelming grief which brought this entire city to a standstill in the days following an unthinkable disaster which could so easily have destroyed one of the world's great football clubs.

What I couldn't tell the Glazers is what impact Munich had on both the families of those who died in that air-crash and the families of those who survived. I believe the Glazer brothers would welcome that information. The Munich disaster, as tragic as it was, is an essential part of the history of the club they now own.

Some would say that Munich is THE most essential part in the story of Manchester United.

So on their next visit to this city I would strongly urge one of the Glazer boys to spend £14.99 on a new book - *The Lost Babes: Manchester United and the Forgotten Victims of Munich* - about the Munich disaster which has been written by Mancunian author Jeff Connor and due to be published, fittingly enough, on February 6 - the 48th anniversary of that dreadful day.

Connor has interviewed survivors of the Munich Disaster and the families of those players who either perished in that crash or have since passed away and their stories make painful, and at times, heart-rending reading.

Both the survivors of Munich and the families of those who

survived are still embittered about the way they were treated by United in the aftermath of that disaster.

For what it's worth, I find it difficult to believe that United turned its back on those players and those families who feature so prominently in the book. I prefer to believe that the club were clumsy in their treatment.

It's my belief that in the weeks and months following the Munich crash, officials at Old Trafford didn't know how to handle the situation, because such a situation had never occurred before. There was no compensation culture back in 1958.

Even the insurance cover for the players involved in the crash was woefully inadequate.

United might argue with some justification that any wrongs which were committed against the players and the families involved in the Munich tragedy were righted in 1998 when the Munich testimonial match was played at Old Trafford between a United XI and a European XI

Surviving players and the families of those who died at Munich did benefit financially from that match to the tune of £47,000, which was a tidy sum but not a life-changing one. But even that pay-out has not eased the bitterness of those players and families who still believe to this day that they were, and have, been badly let down by what Old Trafford officials like to refer to as a "family club".

Only yesterday I talked to one of the Munich survivors and he lost no time in reminding me that those pay-outs from the testimonial game in 1998 came out of the pockets of the Manchester public and not from United's coffers.

So, rightly or wrongly amongst the Munich survivors and the families of those who perished, there remains this deep well of bitterness and resentment against a club which they feel turned it's back on them in their greatest hour of need.

The Glazer brothers should read Connor's book about Munich

and its aftermath. They might understand then how much the very name still means and why emotions are still so raw 48 years after the event.

And maybe when they read it, the Glazer boys might feel moved to pour oil on troubled waters. After all, this is now the 50th year since Sir Matt Busby first took his club into Europe. Why not dedicate a match at Old Trafford late this season to the few remaining survivors and the families of those players who died at Munich or who have died since?

Treat the players and those families to a day out at the Theatre of Dreams. Parade them around the pitch to show them that they've not been forgotten because Munich must NEVER be forgotten. How much would it cost the Glazers to put on a day like that? Loose change. And, whatever the cost, if it eases the pain which those survivors and families still clearly feel, it would be worth every penny.

★

21st July 2000

Dear Mr Hince

I have just read for the umpteenth time an article you wrote in the MEN after City won promotion and for the umpteenth time it made me laugh and cry, just as I laughed and cried at Blackburn on May 7th and as I've done whenever I've watched videos of Kennedy scoring the third goal then turning upfield into Joe Royle's arms. Wonderful stuff! Yet I'm not writing just to commend you as your evocative descriptions of a great day and not for publication either, but to ask if you'd consider putting your typewriter to another use in City's service.

As you quite likely know, there's been a bit of a discussion among City fans about those 'Munich' songs mocking the Manchester United plane crash. Do you think you might write something in the run-up to the derby on November 18th that might disuade the Maine Road crowd from this offensive signing? I sense that many Blues don't like it and it could done away with or at least much reduced if the press and the club itslef took a lead.

I was only 8 years old in 1958 but still remember how the whole of Manchester was affected by the news of the Munich disaster. With Roger Byrne and Duncan Edwards, Tommy Taylor and maybe Eddie Colman, England could have won the World Cup in Sweden that year and I still reckon those four better than any City players I've ever seen - Bobby Johnstone and Colin Bell included.

I've been a Blue since 1955 when I saw the Cup Final on our neighbour's TV, the only house in our street with a set, and ran home crying after Newcastle's third goal. Yet I cannot understand why supporters would sing about young men from a rival team losing their lives.

I've heard some say they shouldn't do it becvause Frank Swift had played for City and he died in the crash too but that kind of parochial view isn't the point, is it? I don't understand that lack of historical awareness or perspective - I've had fans tell me it's OK to refer to United fans as 'Munichs' and sing the 'runway' song (which is really sick) because 'they weren't around in 1958' and hating United has become 'part of City's tradition' but I just do not get it.

There will always be morons, I guess, but I do think that a good article from you in November, perhaps in company with something in the fanzines and club programme, could have some effect. Maybe those supporters who dislike the Munich songs could be encouraged to drown them out when they start with shouts of support for the team we love, rather than songs of hate?

All the best,
Ken Corfield
New York

REDS AND BLUES STOOD
UNITED IN CITY OF TEARS

THE History of professional football is simply littered with appalling tragedies.

The heartbreaking crowd disasters at Ibrox, Burnden Park and Hillsborough. The memory of that dreadful fire at Bradford City still haunts me to this day.

But there is one day – one disaster – which still brings tears to my eyes 50 years after it happened.

That day was February 6, 1958 – the day that Matt Busby's magnificent Babes were decimated in the ice and devastation as their plane crashed on take-off at Munich Airport.

I still find it difficult to write about or talk about that black day – but I'll try – in my clumsy way to describe how that tragedy devastated an entire city, Blues as well as Reds.

Supporting football in this city has markedly changed over the last half century.

I was born into a Blue family and remain so to this day. But for me and hundreds of fellow Blues, Manchester United was our second team.

Maine Road one Saturday, Old Trafford the next. And a dream weekend for me and my fellow Blue Mooners, was a win for both Manchester clubs.

Late in 1957 the world-famous Harlem Globetrotters basketball team were touring England and were due to play an exhibition match at Maine Road.

I was 12 years old at the time and saved my pocket money for weeks to be able to afford the admission money to watch the Globetrotters – and it turned out to be an evening I'll never forget.

I was stood behind the goal in the Platt Lane stand and as

the teams were about to come out, I got this inexplicable urge to
look behind me, I nearly fainted when I glanced over my shoulder.
There, in a line, stood the Busby Babes.

Roger Byrne, like me, educated at Burnage Grammar School.

Duncan Edwards - in my book the greatest defender of all-
time. My God, he was enormous. You could see his thigh muscles
bulging through his trousers.

The elegant Liam 'Billy' Whelan. Snake-hips Eddie Coleman.
Pin-up boy David Pegg.

Every last player in Busby's wonderful team was stood inches
behind me - and I didn't have a pen or a piece of paper.

What I did was to compromise. I scoured up and down the
Platt Lane stand until I found what I was looking for - an empty
cigarette packet. I ripped the packet and spread it out.

Then I returned to my spot, took a deep breath and asked
Roger Byrne if he had a pen I could borrow.

He laughed out loud - tousled my hair - and took a fountain
pen out of his inside coat pocket and handed it to me.

From behind my back I took the shabby cigarette packet and
asked him for his autograph. He signed it and immediately passed
the packet along the line. Every single Busby Babe signed their
name.

For more than 30 years, that tatty bit of cardboard was my most
treasured possession.

Many, many times I was offered money in return for those
signatures.

A friend of mine - a United fanatic - in the Eighties offered
me in excess of £1,000. The answer from me was always the same
I wouldn't have sold that precious ciggy packet for all the tea in
China.

One of my greatest regrets was that somehow I've managed to
lose those priceless signatures.

Only weeks after that chance meeting, Matt took his Babes

to Belgrade to play a European Cup tie against Red Star. On the way back their Elizabethan aeroplane made a re-fuelling stop at Munich Airport.

The weather was atrocious, a blinding snowstorm rendered visibility to a matter of feet, within minutes of touching down the wings of the plane were completely iced up.

Two take-off attempts had to be aborted. Sir Matt was later to admit that he was about to instruct the pilot to cancel the flight but he said nothing as the plane thundered down the runway for a fatal third takeoff attempt.

Back in Manchester, the city was unaware of the tragic events unfolding at Munich Airport.

It took hours for the news to filter through - and when it did it was sketchy. A report on the radio confirmed that United's plane had crashed but there were no details of any casualties.

An entire city held its breath and prayed. Each broadcast carried more bad news.

Roger Byrne - dead. David Pegg - dead. Billy Whelan - dead. Seven members of England's greatest ever football team were lying dead in the snow.

To add irony to tragedy the great former City goalkeeper Frank Swift, then a soccer journalist for the *News of the World*, also lost his life in that crash.

I took a bus to the city centre, don't ask me why, and the heart of Manchester had stopped beating.

The centre was packed out with fans reading a special issue of the *Evening News* and you could have heard a pin drop. No one was speaking. It was eerily silent.

Up to that moment I'd kept my emotions in check. But the sight of adult United and City fans with tears running down their faces was too much for me. I burst into tears and it was hours before the sobs subsided.

There was one slight ray of hope among the despair. The

incomparable Duncan Edwards was still alive – badly injured but alive.

Prayers were offered by both sets of fans for Duncan. He was as strong as a lion, indestructible and while he lived on there was this feeling across the city that Manchester United, the club, would somehow recover from this tragedy. Days after the crash came the devastating news that Duncan had died from kidney failure.

I found it difficult to thank God at that moment but at least he spared Matt Busby although I've suspected ever since that the great man must have been emotionally damaged for the remainder of his days after losing eight of his beloved Babes.

Fifty years ago but to me it seems like yesterday that every Mancunian, young and old, blue or red, wept those bitter tears.

I don't know if there is a God and if there is I'm in no rush to meet him.

But if and when I meet my maker, and if there is a heaven, I know that Roger Byrne, Duncan Edwards and the rest of the Busby Babes will be waiting for me.

I'll get their autographs again – and this time I'll have them forever.

I KNOW THE BABES WERE WATCHING

JUST before the two teams made their entrance yesterday, two snowy white birds fluttered across Old Trafford and settled on the roof of the Stretford End stand. I'm no expert in these matters, but I think they were doves – the symbol of peace.

And how appropriate that would be. For this was the peace derby, when both sets of fans stood in silent harmony in memory of the wonderful Busby Babes.

I came to Old Trafford in trepidation, fearing that some cretin pretending to be a City fan would ruin the silence.

But I need not have worried. From the moment Sir Taggart

and Sven led out their teams, I knew there would be no trouble.

The two managers and their teams came out behind a lone piper. That in itself was poignant enough. I knew from that minute that the morons had done us all a favour by staying clear of the Theatre of Dreams.

The silence itself was both heart-warming and heartbreaking. And that was despite an attempt by some idiot apparently letting off a firework outside the ground which hit the South stand.

How wonderful at the end to see Fergie applauding the blue faithful and the United fans applauding their oldest enemy.

Surely this must be the first time in history that United fans have applauded anything remotely blue.

Never have I felt as proud of the supporters of the club I played for and have worshipped for over half a century.

God bless you wonderful Blue Mooners. Your total silence during those 60 seconds brought tears to my eyes. I knew you wouldn't let me and this city of ours down.

It was my imagination playing tricks on me, of course, but, as the players stood there with heads bowed, I thought I saw a shadowy Matt Busby emerge out of the tunnel followed by NINE Babes holding hands.

And, yes, I do mean nine. And I hope I can right a 50-year-old wrong today by encouraging the Reds to add the name Dennis Viollet to their Munich roll of honour.

Dennis was a silky, lethal striker in that glorious Babes team and later became my manager at Crewe Alexandra.

He was a wonderful man, but that's not the reason why I want to see his name in the trophy room at Old Trafford alongside Roger Byrne, Duncan Edwards and the other players who perished on that black day. Because Dennis also "died" in that disaster.

Dennis passed away in America some years ago from a malignant brain tumour.

But the specialists who treated him were convinced that the

tumour was formed on February 6, 1958, when Dennis suffered serious head injuries in the crash.

What Dennis and no one knew at that time was that the injuries sustained at Munich turned into that fatal tumour.

The tumour had gone undetected because it was sited underneath the bone we all have behind our ears.

So how wonderful it would be for his family if Dennis is immortalised as a fallen Busby Babe. It's the least he deserves.

Right through the impeccably observed silence, the words of the poet, Charles Wolfe, came to mind when he was writing about the Burial of Sir John Moore at Corunna.

"Not a sound was heard, not a funeral note, as his corpse to the rampart we hurried."

And so it was at the Theatre of Dreams yesterday. - not a sound was heard, not a funeral note, as we carried in our minds the Busby Babes to the rampart.

I know the Babes were looking down on the ground yesterday and, red or blue, you did them proud.

It would be pointless of me to give a match report here because you'll be reading the views on other pages from Stuart "The Red" Mathieson and Chris "The Blue" Bailey.

But, of course, in all ways, it was a perfect derby for me. Match won, Babes respected, what more could I have wished for?

ASSORTED FANMAIL

Here is a sample of the letters received as a result of my time at the MEN *ranging from the supportive to the abusive...*

11th March 1993

Dear Mr. Hince,

Oh what joy, the silence is deafening and the quality of the journalism has increased enormously. You will have have gathered that this letter takes the form of a 'get well soon card'.

We were devastated to learn that your regular Tuesday night dish of tripe had been taken off the menu. Friends in high places (in other words, the geezer with the prostate) tells us that you have taken to your bed because you can think of nothing sensible to write. Rumour has it that the 'ace City reporter' could not find the right words. Here, we can be of assistance and would refer you to the vocabulary used by your predecessor (mind you, we know what happened to him).

Words such as 'abysmal', 'pathetic', 'unacceptable', readily spring to mind. Your problem is that you have fallen into the trap of thinking that you can only say good things, being an honest kind of guy. This, no doubt, is what caused you great concern, not the fact that your marking system is based on the following premise: 2 for turning up, 2 for wearing a blue shirt, 2 for facing the right way at kick off time and 1 for promising to give 110% effort.

We think you should get off your backside and get back to your office and ring us whenever you are looking for words. We can promise we will always be ready to assist, although, of course, the end result will be that you go the same way as your predecessor.

We assume of course that you have been asking too much of yourself, it must be difficult for a living legend to aspire to such heights. Perhaps you should lower your sights. It is unreasonable to expect to have the impact on the world of journalism as you had playing for City Reserves at Barnsley on a cold, wet Tuesday night, watched by 3 men, one boy and a dog. Perhaps you should not expect to stride the streets of Wapping as you strode, like a colossus, the playing fields of England.

Seriously though, we are 'sick as a parrot' that you are under the weather and will be 'over the moon' when you are back in business. The flowers, sent under separate cover, are for Mrs. Dragon not for you. We think she deserves some reward for putting up with you at home for the next few weeks.

Really seriously though, we do hope that you are soon back in business and look forward to your usual Tuesday night offering.

With warmest regards.

Ken Ramsden (Secretary, Manchester United)

Ken Merritt (Assistant Secretary, Manchester United)

★

Dear scrambled eggs for brains,

They say that there is nothing like a gracious apology - and that was nothing like one!

Did you fall out of your pram on the way to school one day? I can't believe the drivel in this week's column, you have surpassed yourself. "Oldham are a lovely, lovely club run by lovely people". Have you been reading your Dickie Attenborough books again? "They play football as it should be played!" Get back to the doctor and ask him to reduce your dosage for goodness sake.

Just incase it has slipped your notice, the way football should be played is that the successful teams (known as winners) score more goals than they concede - now that's lovely football.

Please don't go into summer exile. My wife won't let me read the Beano or the Dandy.

Ken Ramsden (Manchester United Secretary)

★

16th November 2006

Dear Hincey,

Talk about 'first the good news, now the bad news'

I got a call from Stuart Mathieson on Tuesday to say that Hincey was no longer with us, could I offer a few words of tribute – then I learn that you were only retiring!!!

They say that in football, like most sports, it's all about timing. Only you could hang up your quill in the week when a certain Championship manager expresses some interesting thoughts about the 'weaker sex' –I couldn't wait for your next column.

What I did say about you, but had edited out last night, was that you were more entertaining as a writer than you were a footballer. But those who followed your (mercifully) short career could accuse me of only stating 'the bleedin obvious'.

Half-seriously though, it's a sad day from the *MEN* that its only entertaining sports writer is retiring – there's even less reason to read it now!

Do keep in touch, and if you want to make your final farewell appearance in our press box on the 9th December just give me a call. Hope to see you then. (I'd ask you to do the Cash Dash but suspect you may have difficulty with the 'dash' bit).

With kindest personal regards,

Ken Ramsden (Manchester United Secretary)

★

17th November 2006

Dear Paul,

We were both shocked to read of your retirement from the *Manchester Evening News* where you were definitely a part of the establishment.

It seemed so sudden to us and we thought you were going to take the vacant managerial seat at one of your former clubs, Charlton Athletic. Now that would be a major surprise and make some headlines!

Everyone is sure to miss your column with its comedy and satire. The paper will never be the same and Bernard and his wife will miss your early morning calls!

Seriously though we wish you all the best for your future and you will always be welcome to the Stadium at the matches, just give Bernard a call to make the arrangements. You might even consider joining the Former Players Association!

Best wishes, yours sincerely,

Alistair Mackintosh (Director, Manchester City), Bernard Halford (Secretary, Manchester City)

★

25th September 1996

Dear Mr Hince,

I don't think this constant blasting away at Francis Lee is entirely necessary, certainly not in public. It harms the club and everyone connected with it at a time when this is the very last thing we need.

I understand what he is trying to say because I felt the same way. It isn't just about printing a rosy picture of City to the exclusion of all else, it's about giving the team a lift when it really needs one. Last season, with relegation drawing ever closer, we could have done with a headline or two of encouragement - *Come On City*, or maybe *You Can Do It Blues!* Instead, every back page of the *MEN* seemed to carry reports of squabbles and constant transfer speculation which only served to unsettle players and fans alike.

On the other hand, I think Mr Lee is wrong to criticise your handling of the current malaise affecting the club because the paper is simply echoing the thoughts of the supporters. Which is right, you can't do anything else but report on what is happening at City.

On the subject of bias: When the new kits came out, City's away strip was featured in the sports section with a black and white photograph, the caption of which didn't even mention the colour. United's new home strip was featured on the front page in colour. A pathetic little point to bring up, I know. But it hurts the fans, you make us feel like unimportant second class citizens. Whether intentional or not, that's biased. And don't get me started on Mr Cantona.

I still recall the colour Page 3 spread of him relaxing in a pub while the nauseating story told us just how normal he was and how he must have been really, really provoked to try decapitating someone. You didn't tell it like it was then (HE'S A THUG would've been completely truthful), but you're wasting no time in laying the law down on City. Biased, again. (When I say 'you' I mean the paper in general).

In conclusion: Print *City Are Shite* if you absolutely must, but just try to balance it out. Remember the players are human, it would be nice for them to pick up the Final on Friday night and see a *Go For It, Boys!* headline, God knows their confidence could do with a boost.

That's the kind of support we're looking for from our local paper.

Yours sincerely,
Colin T. Nicholls

★

23rd September 1996

Dear Paul,

Just a wee note from Scotland to say how I now sympathise with the poor punters of Manchester. Not a week will go by without some raving or other from your good self, and what have they done to deserve it? What have you done to deserve it?

Except be one of the best blokes I ever met in the trade. Many, many thanks for all your help over the years and many, many congratulations.

Love to the family,

Sue Mott,

Daily Telegraph

★

Dear Mr Hince,

I have just read your article in Monday night's *Evening News* about Nicky Butt. You call him a 'cobble street fighter'. To quote "a kid brought up in an area of Manchester where cops patrol in pairs and any cat with both ears intacts has to be a stranger."

You also call him a street urchin, giving the impresion that Gorton is a cross between Victorian Ancoats and Whitechapel in London. What his family think of you inferring he was brought up like a street urchin I hate to think. I certainly would not like it if someone implied I had brought my sons up like street urchins.

We do not wear clogs and shawls in Gorton, no matter what you seem to think. As for police walking round in pairs, that is a load of rubbish. you do not even see one policeman walking about never mind two and strange as it may seem we do have cats round here with both ears intact. Unless of course, they are all strangers to this area.

I have lived in Abbey Hey, Gorton for the past 35 years and would be the first to admit it is far from perfect regarding burglaries etc. But would state that the impression you give of Gorton is grossly misleading.

In the future why don't you just stick to writing about sport, instead of trying to belittle the less affluent areas of Manchester.

Yours faithfully,

Mrs E Southern

Abbey Hey, Manchester

Of course being a Gorton lad I could have told Mrs Southern all this was meant as tongue-in-cheek humour...

★

Dear Paul,

Your account of almost meeting Brian Statham was much appreciated, though I understand neither your diffidence in approaching him to shake his hand nor the implication that he seemed to be going unrecognised at Headquarters. Shame on you and all there!

My memory is of visits to the practice ground after school and watching the lone figure of Statham, with half a dozen old cricket balls, bowling at a single stump and hitting it with great regularity. What dedication! For sheer honest accuracy he was the best!

Yours sincerely,
Maurice Taylor

★

Dear Paul,

First of all, congratulations on your elevation, and your reward for years of good honest reporting, and though I am a United ex-season ticket holder, first of all I am a football supporter. At one stage I frequented Maine Road and Old Trafford, on alternate weeks, I have to admit at that time the Blues with Summerbee, Bell and Lee had the upper hand.

Though I can't pretend to be as close as yourself, I don't attend the matches these days, more of an armchair critic, however I would like to see the Blues get their act together, and I'm sure before long, become a force to be reckoned with.

I've always admired your honest reporting and felt that David Meek never achieved that recognition. Praise and criticism should be given to the players on their merits so please don't let them put the gag on.

Secondly Paul, I refer to your article regarding Brian 'George' Statham, an absolute gent. For three years I was the steward at the G.P.O. Club in Quay Street and for years manager of the Stables Club for Granada, and on many, many occasions met Brian in his capacity as rep for Guinness. It was a great pleasure for me. He was such an unassuming character, no pedestal for him, level-headed, a first class gentleman. Having met thousands in my 27 years behind bars, some who think they are gentlemen until they have had a few bevvies, he stands out as a true one.

He was also admired by his colleagues. Their engineer Ray Bell told me he was forever doing charitable unpaid work, unlike Fred Trueman who was making thousands from his after dinner speaking. Although I must admit it was Fred who arranged for a testimonial for Brian after he left Guinness.

Another one of Brian's problems was he couldn't wear an overcoat in the winter. The rheumatism caused by playing cricket year round, following the sun, meant he couldn't stand the pressure on his shoulders.

Now that you've attained 'chief' status, why not pick the phone up, and approach Brian just for a friendly chat, and just as his bowling you'll find he is as straight as a die.

Yours sincerely,

Tony Hobin

EPILOGUE

NOT SO LONG ago I agreed to be interviewed by a novice reporter who was gaining experience working on one of those free-sheets that comes through the letter box and invariably goes straight in the bin.

At one stage he asked me a very good question. Namely, what were the three most vivid memories of my career as a footballer and as a sports reporter and, put on the spot like that, I was at a loss to give him a decent answer.

Where do you start when asked a question like that? My marriage to Sue? The birth of my first child? Being signed by the club you supported all your life? Sue's death at the age of fifty? My second marriage to Anne? And that's just the tip of the iceberg.

So for the purposes of this book I'm going to pick out an event and two stories I wrote which are never far from my mind.

Because of my excesses (smoking and drinking for England) I had often wondered how I would react if I had a heart-attack. On October 22nd 1997 I got my answer.

I woke as usual at 5.45am that day and felt I had a touch of acid indigestion, you know the feeling, a burning sensation that you know would disappear if you could burp.

While I was taking a bath I started feeling shooting pains down my arms and, oddly, in my jaw bone. I knew then that this was much more than indigestion. What surprised me was how calmly I responded, it was almost as though I was outside my body looking at myself.

I performed the usual routine tasks. I woke up my youngest daughter Kim and told her it was time for work, I even fed the cat before getting into the car to drive to the *Evening News* offices.

By the time I got onto the A6 at the traffic lights alongside the Bull's Head in Hazel Grove I could feel my heart bouncing around my rib cage as though it was doing the rumba. I abandoned the plan to drive into Manchester and instead headed for Stepping Hill hospital which, luckily, is only a few hundred yards from where I live.

I parked outside A&E (and got a ticket in the process) and walked up to reception. It was 6.30 am and the waiting room was empty. The woman on reception asked what was wrong and I told her I thought I was having a heart-attack. She smiled and said "I don't think so sweetie but I'll get a nurse".

The pretty dark-haired nurse who came out sat me down on a chair and put one of those gadgets that looks like a clothes-peg on one of my fingers. She took one look at the print-out and all hell broke loose.

"Crash Team!" she screamed and within seconds I was on a bed in the emergency room. I lay there with a nitro-glycerine pill under my tongue, an oxygen mask over my nose and mouth and a central line pumping morphine and other drugs into my blood stream.

After a minute or two a young lady doctor came to my bed-side and said "Mr Hince, you are having a heart-attack" I took my oxygen mask off and burst out laughing, "Doctor, I think I'd worked that one out for myself!"

A brilliant consultant, Mr Lewis, arrived and told me he was going to inject me with an American clot-busting drug that cost £6,000 a shot but nothing happened - my ticker by this point was doing somersaults and back flips. Mr Lewis told me he was going to try something he had never tried before, he was going to inject me with this bog standard British 'clot-buster' that probably cost the NHS a grand total of 50p.

Within seconds of that injection I could feel my heart starting to behave itself. A minute later I felt I could get off that bed and drive to work as though nothing had happened. The consultant put me straight. He told me at one stage he had considered putting me in the specialist heart unit at Wythneshawe Hospital but felt that even in an ambulance I would never have survived the journey.

Like the rest of you I have at times cursed the NHS system. When you've waited 6 hours in the A&E department waiting for someone to look at a dislocated thumb, for instance. But I know now that if you're in serious trouble and your life is in danger our hospital system is the best in the world. Without it you wouldn't be reading this book. I literally I owe the NHS my life and I'll never forget it.

Did that heart attack change my life? Yes. Right up to the moment I left hospital. Then it was back to the Murphy's and the Dunhill International. Do I feel guilty? Absolutely. But without those little pleasures life, for me, wouldn't be worth living.

Now to the two stories I wrote during my time as the Chief sports writer for the *Evening News*. Sifting through the vast number of words I have written over the years I decided to reduce an article's merits to just one criteria. A writer may be entertaining or instructive but are his words ever beneficial to another member of the human race? Well the first example proves that they could be.

In May 1999, I was at Old Trafford for United's decisive match against Spurs, the first leg of what would prove to be ten days during which the Reds clinched the treble. Scanning the programme I was intrigued to see that a young unknown singer by the name of Russell Watson was going to sing 'Nessun Dorma' before the kick-off.

Russell marched onto the pitch with his microphone and no one gave a monkeys. The two sets of fans were still baiting one another as he cleared his throat but but within seconds every single fan was silent.

I sat there in the press box covered in goose pimples and with the hairs on the back of my neck standing to attention as I listened to Russell's amazing voice. "How could a kid from Salford sing like that?" I asked myself, "He has surely been given a gift from God."

I decided to include Russell's performance in my match report, "You know you have just witnessed something special when the cynical hacks in the press box all rise to their feet to join in the ovation. I swear even the pigeons on the roof of the stands flapped their wings".

The next day Russell called and thanked me profusely for the few kind words I had said about him. He believed those words would kick-start his career. We spoke many more times of the next few weeks and every time we spoke he was a bit more famous. I told him that there would come a time when he wouldn't have time for an ageing hack from his local newspaper but he swore that would never happen.

Today, if Russell and I were on the same street and I burst into flames he wouldn't piss on me. Am I surprised or disappointed by this? Neither, that's the way the world is. The famous don't associate with the likes of you and I, so I'll just be grateful that I managed to give him a leg-up when he needed it.

The second story that sticks out from my time on the MEN came from that amazing game at Old Trafford between England and Greece when David Beckham carried us to the 2002 World Cup Finals in Japan on his own back. But what I wrote the following Monday had nothing to do with the match itself. It was about how Beckham took care of the incredibly brave little girl Kirsty Howard.

Kirsty has raised millions for the Francis House Hospice in Manchester. Beckham has young kids of his own and you could see that by the tenderness he showed to Kirsty that day. He genuinely cared for her and seeing a strapping footballer embracing a little poorly waif attached to an oxygen cylinder brought tears to my eyes. At the end of my report I wrote, "Becks, I don't give a hoot whether you're playing for England or Stockport County - as a man and a person you're Premiership Class".

You will see elsewhere in this book the lovely letter I received from the Senior Sister at Francis House in response to my thoughts on Beckham. I phoned Sister Austin to thank her and she asked me to come to the hospice and see the kids for myself. I had to refuse. Seeing young boys and girls with no life expectation would have been too hard to bear.

However, Sister Austin did say that donations had increased significantly since my article appeared in the *News*. So I might - just might - have played a part in extending or saving the life of one of those seriously ill youngsters in Francis House.

If that has happened I will die believing I was put on this planet for a good purpose.

★

FRANCIS LEE COULDN'T stand the sight of me, and the feeling was mutual. If he burst into flames I wouldn't piss on him. The great Colin Bell shares my opinion of Lee. Colin, one of life's good guys, doesn't swear. I've been alongside him when he's been booted into "Row X", and the worst he's ever uttered is "Frigging heck". He told me that if he saw Lee in the street he wouldn't cross over to speak to him.

But it remained obvious that I wouldn't win a battle while Lee remained as City Chairman. So I told my editor, Mike Unger, that it was time I moved on. A City reporter who had no discourse with a City Chairman is about as useful as a flea in a duvet.

So I moved onto other things, while always keeping an eye on my Blessed Blues.

Time passed, and it suddenly dawned on me that my sixtieth

birthday was looming on the horizon. Sixty years old. When I looked in the mirror I looked eighty, but inside I felt like a twenty-year old. But then the mind kicked in. I had left school at sixteen, and now I was sixty. My arithmetic is a bit wonky, but I made that 44 years without ever being out of work. Two life sentences if you put it another way.

So I decided to retire. *The Evening News* had been wonderful employers, but nothing surprised me anymore. I'd been working for so long that every story seemed to be one I'd written before. I suppose you could say that I had become bored.

I thought I would be blissfully happy drinking Murphy's at seven in the morning and smoking for Great Britain. I was wrong. For the first time in my life I've realised that you need a focus in life - a reason to get up in the morning.

So that's why I've written this book. I've no idea whether it's brilliant, average or a pile of shit. What I can say is that if more than ten of you buy these memories I might be tempted to write another one. William Shakespeare said that most people only have one book inside them – but what did he know about writing...

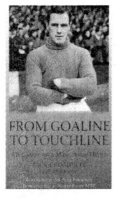